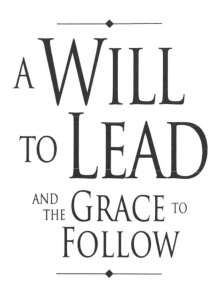

A WILL TO LEAD AND THE GRACE TO FOLLOW

WILLIAM H. WILLIMON

A WILL TO LEAD AND THE GRACE TO FOLLOW

LETTERS ON LEADERSHIP FROM A PECULIAR PROPHET

Edited by Bryan K. Langlands

Abingdon Press
Nashville

A WILL TO LEAD AND THE GRACE TO FOLLOW
LETTERS ON LEADERSHIP FROM A PECULIAR PROPHET

Copyright © 2011 by Abingdon Press

This book is printed on acid-free paper.

Library of Congress Cataloging-in-Publication Data

Willimon, Wiliam H.
   A will to lead and the grace to follow: letters on leadership from a peculiar prophet / William H. Willimon; edited by Brian K. Langlands.
       p.   cm.
   ISBN 978-1-4267-1591-4 (book - pbk. / trade pbk., adhesive—perfect binding : alk. paper)
   1. Christian leadership.   I. Langlands, Brian K.   II. Title.
   BV652.1.W5125 2011
   253—dc22

                                                                            2011014834

11 12 13 14 15 16 17 18 19 20—10 9 8 7 6 5 4 3 2 1

MANUFACTURED IN THE UNITED STATES OF AMERICA

CONTENTS

FOREWORD

I read somewhere, I think it was in an article in the *Harvard Business Review* (What does it tell you that I, a Methodist preacher, am reading the *Harvard Business Review?* It tells me that my church has given me a job for which I have little experience, few qualifications, and no training. Help me!): a leader floods the system with information in the faith that the system has the resources to receive the information and then to do something with it to revive the organization.

As a preacher I've been flooding the system with information for the past four decades—*preaching*. A preacher stands up weekly (and sometimes *weakly*) and pounds the church with images, stories, data, curses, caveats, and pronouncements all in the faith that God will give the church what it needs to take that information and do something faithful with it.

In *faith* (yes, that's the word for it) a Christian communicator tells things to the church and points out problems without the foggiest idea of what to do about it, in faith that God graciously gives the church all it needs to be faithful. I recall the dear, sweet layperson who complained that my sermons "always talk about what's wrong with us without ever giving us anything to do about it."

I responded, in love, "You idiot. That's not my job. I'm called to tell you what's wrong. You are baptized to pray to God to give you the creativity and guts to do something about it." Or as I once heard Robert Schuller put it, "it's my job to dream; it's the laity's job to scheme."

I can't believe I'm quoting Robert Schuller.

Foreword

One of the reasons why my church is in precipitous decline is a lack of information, a paucity of ideas, a failure of intellectual nerve. That's where I come in with my weekly "Bishop's Email" salvos. Not that my ideas are the best ones, but I trust that the Holy Spirit is using my ideas to stimulate their even better ideas. I think it important that the laity see their pastoral leaders as people who are chock full of ideas, brimming over with thoughts, possessed by more sermons than we'll ever be able to preach.

Curiously, when I initiated my weekly email barrage, I thought I was talking with clergy. Very quickly I realized that I tend to get more response, judging by the emails I receive, from the laity. Something like six thousand people now receive these electronic epistles of mine, necessitating about an hour a day spent responding to their responses. By the end of my first year I realized that I had extended conversations, over email, with over four hundred pastors and laity about subjects in the "Bishop's Email." To be sure, email communication leaves something to be desired, but communication is valuable whenever it is about some valuable subject. My basic assumption is that the church is the most valuable thing God ever gave us.

In a job like mine, many conversations tend to degenerate into exclusively institutional, organizational, clergy-centered concerns—Bishop, what are you going to give me next? Bishop, can you relieve me of some of my God-given responsibilities by taking them on your shoulders? Bishop, you are so powerful that you can make all the failures in my ministry turn out right. And so on. My "Bishop's Email" has been a way of giving me and my pastors, with the laity, something more interesting to talk about than ourselves, namely the God who has come to us in Jesus Christ.

All the pieces selected by Bryan for this book are occasional in nature. I am delighted that in these pages these thoughts will live on for a while. Preachers are accustomed to having what we say die quickly after we've said it. Still, my goal in these messages is not some measure of eternality—only God Almighty can give that—but rather being helpful. If what I've said here proves helpful to anyone outside of Alabama, it's a testimony not to my brilliance but to God's ever-active grace. Active grace is the force that moves the planets and the stars, that puts the body of Christ in motion, that keeps dragging us, poor old crucified body that the church always is, into greater faithfulness, in spite of ourselves. Grace, all the way down.

Will Willimon
The Third Sunday in Ordinary Time
2009

INTRODUCTION

Context matters. The older I get the more I appreciate that truth. For the past four years the context in which I have lived, loved, and ministered has been unusual. My primary work involves serving as one of the campus ministers at Georgetown College, which is a small Christian liberal arts college in the bluegrass region of central Kentucky. From 2007 until the summer of 2010, I also served as the pastor of Mt. Gilead United Methodist Church, which is a small, rural congregation nestled among the hills, corn fields, and cattle farms of Scott County, Kentucky.

Every week at Georgetown College I minister with passionate, wild-eyed nineteen-year-olds who have more creativity and love for the Lord than I do. They inspire me, without fail, each and every week of the school year. They give me great hope that even if Christians who are of my generation (Generation X) and older continue to lead mainline churches into decline, even if we continue to hamstring the work of the body of Christ, nevertheless God will provide. After all, the Scriptures remind us that we serve a God who can raise up children out of stones and stoners alike, either with or without our help.

The congregation I led at Mt. Gilead, however, consists of an older community of saints. Although we had some young families and younger folks join the congregation more recently, the majority of that church family is aging. Most of the church members either grew up on a farm or live next to a farm currently.

Unlike most of them, however, I grew up near the beach. My youth was spent surfing and skateboarding, not farming, so I have received an education both in rural living and in God's prodigious Kingdom since becoming the pastor of Mt. Gilead four years ago.

I have learned, for example, how one member grew up on a family farm that was almost entirely self-sufficient. The only things they bought from the store were coffee and sugar. Just about everything else they consumed they either raised, grew, or made themselves. I quickly realized that whereas I am relatively new to the current conversations about sustainability and restraint, many members of this small, off-the-radar church family have been practicing a lifestyle of simplicity and "slow food" that was forged in the crucible of the Great Depression.

Another family in particular comes to mind. Hiddel and June Roman are a middle-aged married couple. Hiddel is originally from Puerto Rico and he was raised in the Pentecostal tradition. He has lived in the U.S. for more than thirty years now and knows the Bible way better than I do. June is a local girl, a special education teacher who preaches each Sunday morning on the local radio station. As a single person, June adopted two special needs children, Michael and Sharon, more than twenty-five years ago. The doctors said that Michael would not live past his first birthday; his life truly is a miracle. Sharon assisted me with serving Holy Communion each month, and I have never met anyone more committed to her ministry.

After adopting Michael and Sharon, June later married a man named Bill. Sadly, Bill died several years into the marriage after suffering a massive heart attack. A few years later, during some of the worst flooding that this region has ever seen, June met a man named Hiddel on the internet. Through a series of improbable events that had God's fingerprints all over them, the couple met two weeks later in New York City and were married shortly thereafter. Hiddel moved from Coney Island to live with his new bride June, Michael, and Sharon in Harrison County, Kentucky, just across the border from Scott County. The Roman family is involved with three different church families, including a

Hispanic church plant. The entire family has covenanted with God to discern God's will and direction for their lives; currently, that includes discerning a possible calling to full-time ministry.

Serving with this family for three years reminded me of something I heard and read about in seminary, namely, that following Jesus Christ faithfully is an unbridled adventure full of risks and unexpected grace. As much as we church folks (especially we clergy) may domesticate the gospel and inoculate one another from the infectious and invasive Holy Spirit, that same Spirit refuses to be leashed. The Spirit infiltrates and Jesus leads and the Father beckons those who have heard the calling to lose their life in order to find it.

In my work as the pastor of Mt. Gilead, I was charged with guiding (where the Spirit led) a platoon of justified sinners in an age of cultural flux and transition. Since we sometimes found ourselves tracking the Spirit off of the beaten path through the fog of a new day dawning, we needed landmarks and signs that would help us to discover the way forward. Fortunately, about the same time that I became the pastor of Mt. Gilead I also discovered Bishop Willimon's weekly messages and subscribed to receive them each week. I have found these weekly messages to be efficacious guides that helped me and the laity: to learn from the successes of other small churches, to become more aware of current leadership, ecclesial, and sociological trends, and to encounter the God who is let loose in this world.

Bishop Willimon's messages have served as challenging and timely reminders that because the God we serve is on the move the body of Christ cannot stand still. Since stagnation equals decline and death, the body of Christ must move, toddling and traversing forward, wearing the dust from the footsteps of her Lord. To help propel that small congregation, I used these messages as devotions in church council meetings, as lessons in Sunday school classes, and as fodder for individual conversations and for preaching. These weekly messages have informed and encouraged my ministry so much that my hope in helping to bring them to publication is that more pastors and lay folks will read them and be similarly challenged, equipped, and empowered.

From among the nearly three hundred weekly messages that Bishop Willimon has dispatched since moving to Alabama, we have culled for this volume the most relevant, the sharpest, and the most broadly applicable. Rather than arranging them chronologically according to the date of composition, we have organized these selected messages into chapters comprising of messages that are thematically linked. The messages contained in this volume cover a wide range of topics: consumerism and culture, small church revitalization, women and ministry, theological politics, church planting, and the emerging generation, to name but a few. Although these messages are categorized thematically into chapters, there is definite cross-pollination throughout the volume. Thus, for example, even though there is a chapter on Easter and a chapter on Women and Ministry, one will inevitably discover descriptions and examples of resurrection in the stories about women and ministry that Willimon highlights.

I was blessed to serve as a teaching assistant for (then Dean) Willimon back at Duke Divinity School in 2003 and 2004. Perhaps what I have always appreciated most about his ministry is his constant reminder that to join up with Jesus Christ is to commit to the *adventure* of God's good news. As there is nothing tame, tepid, or sanitary about the ministry, passion, or resurrection of Jesus Christ, I have found Bishop Willimon's weekly teachings to be the kind of constant, grounded, and wise provocation that I need in order to preach and minister with more courage, candor, and conviction than I naturally have. Thanks be to God for blessing the body of Christ with seasoned voices who inspire young, precocious, and naive preachers like me. Whether you are a pastor, a lay person, a seeker, or a skeptic, my prayer for you is that the Holy Spirit will move, disrupt, invade, provoke, inspire, overwhelm, and humble you in beautiful ways through these collected messages.

Bryan K. Langlands
Fourth Sunday after Pentecost
2010

CHAPTER 1

ADVENT AND CHRISTMAS

THE CHALLENGE OF ADVENT

After my first Advent/Christmas at the university chapel where I used to preach, I noted that sermons during this season frequently received negative responses from some in the congregation. What's the problem? Is not this a prelude to one of the Christian year's most joyous seasons?

One person emerged after I had preached at the Advent service at another university chapel and accused me of "promoting irresponsible passivity" in my sermon. "You should remind us," he said, "that we are educated, responsible people who have been given the gifts to make the world a better place."

Yet what was I to preach, stuck as I was with the repeated Advent gospel assertion that God really has come in Jesus Christ to do for us what we could not do for ourselves? How could I calibrate the Hebrew Scriptures' prophetic announcement that history had again become interesting not because we had at last gotten organized but because God was moving among us? In short, my critic had gotten more than a whiff of eschatology and found its odor distinctly offensive to his activist, educated, progressive sensibilities. He, like most of us, would rather get better than be born again. He, like most of us, wants a world improved rather than a world made new.

Advent is the season of "the last (Greek: *eschatos*) things," a time of winter death in nature, the ending of another year. Yet it is also the beginning of the church year, a time of birth at Bethlehem, a time when we know not whether to name what is happening among us as "ending" or "beginning," for it feels both as if something old is dying and as if something new is being born.

Christian eschatology, like Jewish eschatology before it, makes a claim about the future in which the Creator of the world at the beginning is fully revealed as the world's Redeemer at the end. Eschatology is more a matter of Who? than When? "The end" is not so much a matter of chronology (when?) but rather a debate over who, in the end, is in charge. The hope for the coming of Christ in fullness (Christ's *parousia*) has nothing to do with the hope engendered by wishful thinking, a positive mental attitude, or creative social programming.

Advent promises us that, when all has been said and done by God, in us as individuals, in our political/social/economic structures, in the whole cosmos, God will reign. What God is doing among us, for us, often despite us is large, cosmic, political— nothing less than "a new heaven and a new earth" (Revelation 21:1).

Our individual hope is grounded in the promised cosmic dismantling and reconstructive transformation that God is doing in the whole world. John Howard Yoder was pointing to the eschatological nature of our hope when he suggested that the word "revolution" was a bit closer to the root meaning of *euangelion* than merely "good news." The good news of Advent is that we are being met, reconstructed by a God who intends to make all things new.

President Bush stood before Congress and, paraphrasing a beloved old hymn, said, "there is power, wonderworking power in . . . the good American people." That's not a Christian belief.

More than likely, Advent eschatology offends us for more mundane reasons. I am at church seeking personal advice for how to have a happy marriage or how to get along with the boss next week, only to have Advent wrench my gaze away from my subjectivity with its insistence that whatever God is about in the Advent of Jesus, it is something quite large, quite cosmic, quite strange and humanly unmanageable, something more significant than me. I am not the master of history.

So let us begin with the honest admission that our real problem with these Advent/Christmas texts is largely political and economic. Tell me, "This world is ending. God has little vested interest in the present order," and I shall hear it as bad news.

However, for a mother in a barrio in Mexico City who has lost four of her six children to starvation, to hear that, "This present world is not what God had in mind. God is not finished. Indeed, God is now moving to break down and to rebuild in Jesus"; I presume that would sound something like gospel. For her the Advent/Christmas message presages a revolutionary conflagration.

A great deal depends, in regard to our receptivity to these texts, on where we happen to be standing at the time when we get the news, "God is coming."

It's Advent. Let the revolution begin. (December 3, 2007)

IN THE DARKNESS, A VOICE, A LIGHT

John 1:6-9, 19-23

> There was a man sent from God, whose name was John. He came as a witness to testify to the light, so that all might believe through him. (John 1:6-7)

As a child, I was frightened of the dark. I grew up in a rural area and, when it was dark, it was really dark—no street lamps, no passing automobiles. Dark. How well I remember that long walk, which I would have to make, down our winding drive through the pine trees from the highway to our house. At the end of the drive, though, as I came in sight of the house lights, there was often my mother's reassuring, "Is that you?"

Nothing tames the terrors of the darkness like a light, a voice.

John's Gospel opens by saying, "The people who sat in darkness have seen a great light." Israel was in darkness, the dark of political oppression. Judea was occupied by Rome. These are the people upon whom light has shined, says John. But before there was light, there was a voice, a voice in the darkness. That voice belonged to John, John the Baptist. John the Baptist is the voice who proclaims a light coming into the darkness.

All the Gospels tell about John. And yet we get most of our detailed information about John from Matthew and Luke. They tell that he ate insects, lived in the desert, and wore camel hair. Strange. John's Gospel tells us none of this. All John tells us is that John the Baptist was "a voice." We have to figure out who he is and what he is up to by what John says.

People ask, "Who are you?" John tells them that he is a mere forerunner. John also waits. He says that the one for whom he is preparing the way is one who is great. But John doesn't seem to know many details. He only knows that his coming will be light in the darkness, that great advent people are expecting.

We have sung advent hymns of waiting, "Come, Thou Long Expected Jesus." "O Come, O Come, Emmanuel." Waiting is not easy for us. Waiting is particularly difficult when we are waiting in the dark, when we can't see the way forward, when there is no reassuring light and we do not know whether we are going forward or backward.

One feels so vulnerable in the dark. We like to be in control. We like to know that we are taking sure steps forward, meeting our goals, getting somewhere. But in the dark, one is unsure. One stumbles. And I don't like to stumble.

Oddly, sometimes people speak of the Christian life as fulfillment. "Now I have found Jesus." "Now I have gotten my life together." "Now I have turned myself over to God and I am saved." It sounds like it's all finished, done, complete, fulfilled. But so much of the Christian life is spent waiting, yearning, leaning forward to that which we need but do not yet have.

What are you waiting for? We speak too negatively of waiting. Show me a person who is not waiting, not yearning, not leaning forward, not standing on tiptoes hoping for something better and

I will show you a person who has given up hope for anything better, someone who has settled down too comfortably in present arrangements.

And that's part of the message of John the Baptist. His was a voice, a voice speaking into our darkness, telling us that there is dawn. He was a watchman, standing on the starlit hill, looking east, telling others that it was almost day.

Beyond, behind our deepest longing and yearning, that is really what we want. Our times of darkness are vivid reminders that we are, in truth, frail, vulnerable, and needy. We really are those who need deliverance. And our deliverance has got to be something beyond ourselves, someone greater than our own abilities to deliver.

John did not know the complete shape of that hope. John was a voice, a voice into the darkness, telling people not to give up hope, telling people that their yearning was not mere wishful thinking, that their longing was an act of faith, a deep and abiding belief that God cared, that God would come and deliver.

You may have read Viktor Frankl's classic account of his experiences in a Nazi death camp, *Man's Search for Meaning*. Frankl had been a successful therapist. While in the camp, he spent his time observing himself and his fellow inmates. Frankl noted that some of the prisoners just wasted away and died quickly, even though they had no discernable physical ailments. He recalls one man who was doing reasonably well, considering the deplorable conditions of the camp. The man often talked of his dream to get out of the camp and to be united with his dear wife. Then the man received word that his wife had died in another prison camp. And in just a couple of days, the man died.

Frankl concluded that the man died, not because of some bodily ailment, not because he lacked food or water, but because he lacked hope. He lacked hope that there was anything to be had beyond the darkness of the bleak prison, that there was anything beyond the present anguish of Nazi brutality. We can live, said Frankl, longer without bread than we can live without hope.

Hope that the light shines in the darkness.

We gather on this night as those who yearn, who desire, who are not yet fulfilled, but who are confident that light breaks into the darkness, and we shall see, and we shall know, and we shall be filled.

The light, the world's light, our light, has a face, a name—Emmanuel. (December 17, 2007)

CHRISTMAS IN THE EMPIRE

On Christmas Eve we read a story about how a poor couple named Mary and Joseph were forced by imperial political decrees to pack up, to journey across the countryside (even though Mary was expecting a baby), to hole up in a cow stable, all as the result of Caesar's enrollment. The Romans had the most power and the biggest army of any Western country ever to conquer the Middle East. How are you going to keep these Jews in their place if you don't enroll them? So Caesar Augustus decreed, and cruel King Herod enforced the order that everybody had to go to the city of his or her ancestors and get registered. Mary and Joseph were Jews, under the heel of the vast Roman Empire, the greatest empire the world has ever known, with the largest army of occupation—that is, until us.

When I read the Christmas story, it is unfair for me to read myself into the places of Mary and Joseph, the shepherds, or even the wise men. This was their home. They are under the heel of the empire, their lives jerked around by imperial decrees.

I live in Rome with Caesar Augustus, or maybe in Jerusalem up at the palace with that King Herod, lackey for the Roman overlords. I'd rather see myself as one of the relatives of Mary and Joseph. I wouldn't mind being one of the shepherds, out working the night shift, surprised when the heavens filled with angels.

But that is not my place in the story. My place in the story is as a beneficiary of the empire. I am well fixed. I don't live up in the palace, but I live in a home which—with its modern conveniences and security—the majority of the world's people would call a palace. I have been the beneficiary of a great classical education, and I am a citizen of a country that has dominated other countries, often without even trying to dominate other countries. We are the empire.

I don't like my particular place in the story of the first Christmas.

So when you think about it, in our context, it is odd in a way that so many of us should flock to church on a Christmas Eve. It is a bit strange that we should think that, in Christmas, we hear such unadulterated good news, that we should feel such warm feelings, and think that we are closer to God now than at any other time of the year.

I guess we ought to be of the same frame of mind as our cousin, King Herod. When he heard the word about the first Christmas, the Gospels say that he was filled with fear. Give Herod credit. He knew bad news when he heard it. He knew that the songs that the angels sang meant an attack upon his world, God taking sides with those on the margins, the people in the night out in the fields, the oppressed and the lowly.

But for the people up at the palace, the well fixed, the people on top, the masters of the empire, Christmas was bad news. And many of them were perceptive enough to know it.

So maybe that is why we cover up Christmas with cheap sentimentality, turn it into a saccharine celebration. Maybe, in our heart of hearts, we know that Christmas means that God may not be with the empire, but rather the empire may be on a shaky foundation, and that if we told the story straight, as the Bible tells it, we might have reason, like Herod (when he heard about the first Christmas) to fear.

Let us hear again the song of the angels:

> But the angel said to them, "Do not be afraid; for see—I am bringing you good news of great joy for all the people." (Luke 2:10)

The angel did not say good news for some people. The angel was bold to say good news for *all people*. All. Though the angel was singing to the shepherds, the angel meant the song for everybody. Herod no doubt had difficulty hearing the song, safely fortified as he was with his troops and his thick-walled palace. Herod, the old fox, missed it.

But you haven't missed it. Even though you are a card-carrying member (as am I) of the greatest empire that has ever ruled, you are in the right place to hear the news. Good news this day. There is born for you a savior. Our flags, government, armies, cannot save. Only that baby saves. One who is born among the lowly and the poor—only that one saves.

He comes not only for the oppressed, not only for Israel, but for the oppressor, that is, for all. O that we in the empire could hear that song, O that we could turn back to the Lord, change our ways, bow down before the manger, rather than before our power, acknowledge our need, and pledge allegiance to the Prince of Peace.

Because he is our prince too. He comes to form an empire unlike the way this world builds empires; it's called the kingdom of God. And he shall reign forever and ever, and of his reign there shall be no end.

Good news. For this day in the city of David is born a Savior, Christ the Lord. Good news *for all*. Amen. (December 24, 2007)

CHRISTMAS MEDITATION

Throughout the churches of North Alabama United Methodism, we are preparing to celebrate the mystery of the Incarnation. The proclamation that God became flesh and moved in with us (John 1) is one of the most distinctive affirmations of the Christian faith, perhaps the most distinctive. Comparison with other accounts of who God is and what God does is instructive.

In Islam, at least from my amateurish reading of the Koran, there is this constant distancing of God, apparently as a means of honoring God. The view of God that emerges in the Koran is noble and exalted, but God is clearly at some remove from the world. God is as absolute, as majestic as God can get. You would have to know the Christmas story to know why that's a problem.

Christians don't know that God is sovereign, noble, exalted, absolute, high and lifted up. We know that God is in the world, with us, for us, Emmanuel. Jesus is a prophet, but prophets, even the most truthful and courageous of them, cannot save. When we see God next to us, stooped toward us, in the muck and mire with us in order to save us, that's what we call sovereign, noble, and exalted.

A story: A man died. He had not lived the most worthy of lives, to tell the truth. In fact, he was somewhat of a scoundrel. He therefore found himself in hell, after his departure from this life. His friends, concerned about his sad, though well-deserved fate, went down to hell, and moved by the man's misery, rattled those iron gates, calling out to whomever might be listening, "Let him out! Let him out!"

Alas, their entreaties accomplished nothing. The great iron doors remained locked shut.

Distinguished dignitaries were summoned, powerful people, academics, intellectuals, prominent personalities. All of them stood at the gates and put forth various reasons why the man should be let out of his place of lonely torment. Some said that due process had not been followed in the man's eternal sentence. Others appealed to Satan's sense of fair play and compassion. The great iron gates refused to move.

In desperation, the man's pastor was summoned. The pastor came down to the gates of hell, fully vested as if he were to lead a Sunday service. "Let him out! He was not such a bad chap after all. Once he contributed to the church building fund and twice he served meals at a soup kitchen for the homeless. Let him out!" Still, the gates of hell stood fast.

Then, after all the friends and well wishers finally departed in dejection, the man's aged mother appeared at the gates of hell.

She stood there, stooped and weak, only able to whisper softly, in maternal love, "Let *me* in."

And immediately the great gates of hell swung open and the condemned man was free.

Something akin to that great miracle happened for us on a starry night at Bethlehem. (December 18, 2006)

CHAPTER 2

TO EASTER

NO MORE OF THIS! A MEDITATION FOR HOLY WEEK

Luke 22:35-38, 47-51

The story of Jesus' Passion ends in high drama, and not just in the movies. At last the moment comes for the soldiers to arrest Jesus. And at that moment the disciples ask Jesus a curious question: "Lord, should we strike with the sword?" (Luke 22:49). It is curious, because, well, these are the disciples, the ones closest to Jesus. What of that which Jesus taught or did up to this point would lead the disciples to think that now they should strike with the sword?

There is a somber irony here. When Jesus is arrested the soldiers have swords. No irony in that, of course; all soldiers have swords. This is the way governments work, with swords. This is the way we attain national security, with swords. As you pay taxes this year, for the largest military budget in the world, know that all that "In God We Trust" talk is not exactly true: in a pinch, give us a good sword.

The irony is that *Jesus' own disciples have swords.* Matthew, Mark, and Luke don't name the disciple with the sword. John says that the sword-swinging disciple was none other than Peter, the rock, the church, *us*.

All of that Jesus talk about turning the other cheek, about not resisting evil, was fine for sunnier days, back on the road, when Jesus was popular and spiritual. But when it's dark, as the soldiers come with their swords, it's time for the church to be responsible, to be realistic, to take matters in hand, to take up the sword. Church, let's roll!

Here the people who have heard every word Jesus spoke, seen all of his acts, still ask, "Lord, now shall we strike with the sword?" Even at this point, when Jesus' life is threatened, when his movement is faced with extinction, even then, to our question about perfectly justified self-defense, Jesus replies in no uncertain terms, "Put your sword back into its place; for all who take the sword will perish by the sword" (Matthew 26:52). These are the last words, the very last words, that the disciples hear before they flee into the darkness. Put away the swords.

Surely, if there were ever a moment in human history when violence would be justified, it is here when the Son of God is being so unjustly attacked. But then come the words of Jesus: "No more of this." Jesus is against swords because of something Jesus knows about God. The authorities have their swords that prop them up. Jesus has nothing to support his kingdom but God. Yet sadly, the disciples of Jesus are propped up with swords. "No more of this!" (Luke 22:51).

When we draw the sword, there is no difference between the empire and us. The state is careful to identify its enemies, to get conclusive evidence against them, as justification for its violence. Jesus commands us to love our enemies, to take our swords and beat them into plows.

At this, his final word to them, his last command, the disciples of Jesus run away into the dark. And Jesus is left alone, to go head-to-head with the powers. He is led like a lamb to the slaughter. And we, with swords in our hands, flee to darkness. And the Christian faith claims that this is the way God wins God's victories!

Back when I was at the university, during Islamic Awareness Week, we had a panel. There was an imam from Chicago, a local rabbi, and me (representing all Christians everywhere, even though you didn't vote for me). During the discussion, the imam said, "Islam is a very tolerant faith. In the Holy Koran, if an unbeliever attacks a believer, I am under obligation to punish the unbeliever. If my brother here, the Jew, is attacked by an unbeliever, the Holy Prophet commands me to punish the attacker." The rabbi seemed pleased by this. For my part, I said, "Gee, I wish Jesus had said that. I've got people I want to punish, folks who need killing. Unfortunately, even when we tried to defend Jesus, he cursed us!"

On the cross, his crucifiers screamed, "He trusted God, let God deliver him." We can't. We may say, on our money, "In God we trust," but when push comes to shove, we ask, "Lord, is now the time to strike with the sword?"

In just a short time, we are going to see that when Jesus says, "In God I trust," he means it. (April 10, 2006)

THE VIOLENT BEAR IT AWAY

A Meditation for Maundy Thursday

Tonight we begin the enactment of a story, Jesus' last hours. I don't know what most impresses you about the story of the arrest, the trial, the crucifixion of Jesus. What impresses me is its sheer bloodiness, the violence. I pray to God that I'll never get so hardened of heart, so inoculated to the violence, that I cease to flinch as Jesus is nailed to the wood.

It's a very violent story. Jesus foretold this night in a parable (Matthew 21). A man had a vineyard. He improved it, built a wall around it, a tower too. He leased his vineyard to some tenants, allowing them to collect and keep the fruit of the vineyard, never charging them rent. One day, he sent his servants to the tenants to collect the rent that was due. The wicked tenants beat the servants, killing one, stoning another half to death. The owner thought, "Unbelievable! This time I'll send my own son to collect my rent. That will surely shame them, or bring out the best in them."

The owner failed fully to reckon the depth of wickedness, the potential for violence among the tenants. They said to themselves, "Well, here comes the son, the heir to the vineyard. Let's bash in his head, kill him, so that it will be ours."

And Jesus says, the kingdom of God is just like that. He who never one time used violence or even self-defense (wouldn't let us use our swords tonight to protect him), was the cause of violence. He, who embodied the best, brought out in us the worst. The gospel is a violent story.

So is ours. We are a violent people, we tenants of the vineyard, and most of the stories about us, if they are true, are bathed in blood. Historian Stephen Ambrose says that 1945, the year before my birth, may have been history's bloodiest year. In every corner of the world, the sight, says Ambrose, of a half dozen teenaged boys, walking down a street, would strike fear among the people. They were armed to the teeth, young killers in uniforms provided by old men in government. I was born one year later, the year of the last lynching in the South, in my hometown. I was conceived in blood.

And weren't we all? Creation is but six chapters old, says Genesis (6:11), when God notes that something had gone terribly wrong. The earth that God intended to be filled with birds and beasts and humanity is "filled with violence."

And hasn't it always been that way, at least in our part of the earth? A three-volume book was published a few years ago entitled *Violence in America*.[1] A brief perusal proves it really is as American as apple pie. We were born in blood, what we call "The Revolution" and others call the genocide of the natives. Consider: 168 people killed by a young man, U.S. Army–trained, in Oklahoma City. The crazed Unabomber, a Harvard man. Most of our children have seen about a thousand TV murders by the time they are ten. And so many of our heroes—Kennedy, King, Lincoln—assassinated by their fellow citizens. I confess I only made it through about twenty of the encyclopedia's nearly two thousand bloody pages.

And he gathered us, the night before he was whipped, beaten, and nailed to the wood. And taking the bread he said, "This is my body, broken, for you." And then the cup, "This is my blood, shed, for you." For you. Because if there were not some blood to it, some brokenness, it wouldn't be for me, for you.

"We don't really believe that the cup actually contains the blood of Christ, do we?" someone asked. Well, why not? What did you think it meant when it said, on Christmas, that "the Word became flesh and moved in with us"?

"I will, having failed at all else, send them the Son," said the Father. That will bring out the best in them, shame them, change them, surely. Well, tonight we see that he came into the world (the world, in the words of Genesis, "filled with violence"), and brought out the worst in us. Any Savior who wants to save us must be willing to get bloody in order to get to us, for our story is one of broken bodies and shed blood.

Earlier, in Matthew's Gospel, when they came and told Jesus that John the Baptist had been arrested and was awaiting execution (Matthew 11:12), Jesus commented that since the first days of Creation, since Genesis, and even since John, the kingdom of heaven has suffered violence, and the violent try to take it by force.

What's new? Well, what's new is this night, that the kingdom should come to us, the violent, not by violence, but by One willing to turn his cheek to the smiters, to shed blood, to allow his body to be broken, for us, for us. (April 5, 2007)

WHILE IT WAS STILL DARK

Early on the first day of the week, while it was still dark, Mary Magdalene came to the tomb and saw that the stone had been removed from the tomb. (John 20:1)

Easter is about brightness and light. Spring colors, nothing drab or dark. But John says that Mary went to the tomb while it was still dark. Things were dark in more ways than one. Mary's world had been plunged into darkness by Jesus' death. Night fell about her, and the darkness invaded her heart.

And on Easter, the last thing in the world she expected happened. Mary Magdalene went to the tomb while it was still dark, and the *resurrection had already happened*. The resurrection of Jesus occurred at night, not in the brightness of day. This is not unprecedented. In the beginning, in Genesis 1, God's first creative act was in the dark. Darkness was upon the face of the deep and the spirit of God was moving over the face of the waters. And God said, "Let there be light." Doesn't all life begin in the dark, in some utterly dark womb? Nobody's ever seen a creation or a resurrection, because God works in the dark.

When you have experienced resurrection, hasn't it been in the dark? God seems not to perform many resurrections on church picnics or Easter Sunday mornings. God works the night shift. And that's good because we do not live in some perennial bright Easter morning. Your spiritual world is not a place where the sun is always shining and the news is always good.

So when bright Easter is done, in your bright, Sunday service at church, remember to expect God whenever it gets dark. When we get to where the road runs out, when the sky turns to midnight at midday, when even the stars forsake us and fall, when our last best hope has been sealed in a tomb, and when three days later it is still dark, then we, by the grace of a living God, may have arrived with Mary Magdalene, surprised by Easter, surprised by God with us, even when, especially when, it's dark. Thanks be to God! Happy Easter. (April 16, 2006)

HE CAME BACK . . . TO US!

And very early on the first day of the week, when the sun had risen, they went to the tomb. . . . As they entered the tomb, they saw a young man, dressed in a white robe, . . . [and] he said

to them, "Do not be alarmed; you are looking for Jesus of
Nazareth, who was crucified. He has been raised; . . . he is going
ahead of you to Galilee; there you will see him, just as he told
you." (Mark 16:2-7)

Mark says that on that first Easter, women went to the tomb to
pay their last respects to poor, dead Jesus. To their alarm, the
body of Jesus was not there. A "young man, dressed in a white
robe," told them, "You are looking for Jesus of Nazareth, who was
crucified? Well, he isn't here. He is raised. He is going ahead of
you to Galilee."

Here's my Easter question for you: Why Galilee? *Galilee?*
Galilee is a forlorn, out-of-the-way sort of place. And Nazareth,
a no-count town in south-central Galilee, was where Jesus came
from (which in itself was a shock—in the words of Nathanael,
"Can anything good come out of Nazareth?"—John 1:46a). Jesus
is Galilee's only claim to fame. Jesus spent most of his ministry
out in Galilee, the bucolic outback of Judea. He expended most
of his teaching trying to prepare his forlorn disciples for their trip
up to Jerusalem where the real action was. All of Jesus' disciples
seem to have hailed from out in Galilee.

Jesus' ultimate goal seemed to focus not on Galilee but rather
on the capital city, Jerusalem. In Jerusalem he was crucified and
in Jerusalem he rose. Pious believers in Jesus' day expected a
restoration of Jerusalem in which Messiah would again make the
Holy City the power center that it deserved to be, the capital city
of the world. Which makes all the more odd that the moment he
rose from the dead, says today's Gospel, Jesus left the big city and
headed back to Galilee. Why?

One might have thought that on the first day of his resurrected
life, the risen Christ would have made straight for the palace, the
seat of Roman power, appeared there, and said, "Pilate, you made
a big mistake. Now, it's payback time!"

One might have thought that Jesus would have done something effective. If you want to have maximum results, don't waste
your time talking to the first person whom you meet on the
street; figure out a way to get to the movers and the shakers, the

influential and the newsmakers, those who have some power and prestige. If you really want to promote change, go to the top.

I recall an official of the National Council of Churches who, when asked why the council had fallen on hard times and appeared to have so little influence, replied, "The Bush Administration has refused to welcome us to the White House." How on earth can we get anything done if the most powerful person on earth won't receive us at the White House?

But Jesus? He didn't go up to the palace, the White House, the Kremlin, or Downing Street. (Jesus never got on well with politicians.) Jesus went outback, back to Galilee. Why Galilee? Nobody special lived in Galilee, nobody except the followers of Jesus. Us.

The resurrected Christ came back to and appeared before the very same rag-tag group of failures who so disappointed him, misunderstood him, forsook him, and fled into the darkness. He returned to his betrayers. He returns to us.

It would have been news enough that Christ had died, but the good news was that he died for us. As Paul said elsewhere, one of us might be willing to die for a really good person, but Christ shows that he is not one of us by his willingness to die for sinners like us. His response to our sinful antics was not to punish or judge us. Rather, he came back to us, flooding our flat world not with the wrath that we deserved but with his vivid presence that we did not deserve.

It would have been news enough that Christ rose from the dead, but the good news was that he rose for us.

That first Easter, nobody actually saw Jesus rise from the dead. They saw him afterwards. They didn't appear to him; he appeared to them. Us. In the Bible, the "proof" of the resurrection is not the absence of Jesus' body from the tomb; it's the presence of Jesus to his followers. The gospel message of the resurrection is not first, "Though we die, we shall one day return to life," it is, "Though we were dead, Jesus returned to us."

If it was difficult to believe that Jesus was raised from the dead, it must have been almost impossible to believe that he was raised and returned to us. The result of Easter, the product of the

18

Resurrection of Christ, is the church—a community of people with nothing more to convene us than that the risen Christ came back to us. That's our only claim, our only hope. He came back to Galilee. He came back to us.

In life, in death, in any life beyond death, this is our great hope and our great commission. Hallelujah! Go! Tell! The risen Christ came back to Birmingham, uh, I mean, Galilee. (April 14, 2008)

THE LAST TO BELIEVE IN EASTER

Preparing to preach on Easter I note some curious truths. The first to experience Easter, and the first to preach Easter, were women (take that, those who think that women preaching isn't "biblical"!). And to whom do the women preach the resurrection? The disciples of Jesus.

Preachers and lay leaders of the church please note: the disciples don't believe the women. They think they are hysterical. The disciples dismiss their news as "an idle tale." As Kierkegaard noted, how curious that those who were closest to this event, those whom Jesus had been carefully preparing—his own inner circle, the disciples—are the least prepared to believe. Those who were the most prepared, who had a front row seat in the class—Jesus' disciples—were as dumb as anyone; dumber, actually.

People who teach in theological schools take note: even the two Jewish religious groups who at the time were the most sophisticated in thinking about resurrection, who were working most diligently from the Scriptures to prepare an adequate theological foundation for the resurrection—the Pharisees and the Essenes—missed the whole thing. As Karl Barth once said, when it comes to the gospel, everybody is an amateur, everyone a beginner.

Luke makes the intellectually marginalized—in this case, women, who were denied participation in the educational systems of the day—play a prominent role in our perception of the resurrection. Mary Magdalene—maybe the most marginal of any of the early followers of Jesus—is the chief resurrection witness and the only person to appear in all four accounts. All we know about Mary Magdalene before she joined Jesus is that she had previously been possessed by "seven devils." The "seven devils" could refer to an utterly dissolute moral life or to an extreme form of mental illness. Either or both of these pre-Jesus conditions, coupled with being a woman in a patriarchal society, put her at the far edge of marginality.

If you were Luke and trying to convince people of the truth of the resurrection, would you make your chief endorsements come from those whom the majority of people are least likely to believe? Given the importance that we in our society give to celebrity endorsements, it's more than a little disconcerting that the main witness to the resurrection is a woman on the margins.

Unless that was exactly how it happened. Here is a God who tends to work the margins rather than the center, who does not limit divine revelation to the "in crowd." (You can't get much more in the center of the "in crowd" of the church than being a bishop, and a male bishop at that.)

I think in this early testimony to the resurrection that we read in the Gospels, a parable is here for us, all of us in the church, Jesus' closest friends, the Jesus "in crowd." We may be the slowest to apprehend the full, frightening, wonderful truth of the resurrection. We may have to listen to the testimony of those whom we don't consider to be in the "in crowd." We may have to admit that the resurrection is both our hope and our judgment as followers of Jesus.

Happy Easter. He is risen; he is risen indeed. (April 8, 2007)

NOTE

1. Ronald Gottesman and Richard Maxwell Brown, *Violence in America: An Encyclopedia* (New York: Charles Scribner's Sons, 2001).

CHAPTER 3

ITERATIONS OF RESURRECTION

THE GOD WHO REFUSED TO BE DONE WITH US

God promised to come, in spite of our sad human history. God vowed to be with us, to show us God's glory, power, and love. That all sounded good until God Almighty dramatically made good on the promise and actually showed up as Jesus of Nazareth, not the vague and thoroughly adorable God whom we expected. Even among Jesus' closest followers, his twelve disciples, there was this strange attraction to him combined with an odd revulsion from him. "Blessed is the one who takes no offense in me," he said. But the things Jesus said and did led many to despise him. On a dark Friday afternoon in Jerusalem that revulsion became bloody repulsion as we nailed Jesus' hands and feet to a cross and hoisted him up naked over a garbage dump outside of town. At last we had done something decisive about Jesus and the God he represented, or so we thought.

Three times Jesus had hinted that his death might not be the end of the drama, yet the thought that anything in the world might be stronger than death was inconceivable to everyone around Jesus, even as it is inconceivable today. (First-century Near Eastern people did not know many things that we know,

but everybody knew that what's dead stays dead.) All of his disciples were quickly resigned to his death. End of story.

It was a good campaign while it lasted, but Jesus had not been
enthroned as the national Messiah, the Savior of Israel. Caesar
had won. Rather than cry, "Crown him!" the crowd had
screamed, "Crucify him!" and stood by gleefully as the Romans
executed Jesus on a cross. Mocking him, the soldiers made a
crown of thorns and shoved it on his head, tacking above the
cross a snide sign, "KING OF THE JEWS." Some king, reigning
from a cross. In about three hours, Jesus died of either suffocation
or loss of blood, depending on whom you talk to.

As is so often the case with a true and living God, our sin was
not the end of the story. Three days after Jesus had been brutally
tortured to death by the government—egged on by a consortium
of religious leaders like me—deserted by his disciples, and then
entombed, a couple of his followers (women) went out in the
early morning darkness to the cemetery. The women went forth,
despite the risk in the predawn darkness, to pay their last respects
to the one who had publicly suffered the most ignominious of
deaths. ("Where were the men who followed Jesus?" you ask.
Let's just say for now that Jesus was never noted for the quality or
courage of his male disciples.)

At the cemetery, the place of rest and peace for the dead, the
earth quaked. The huge stone placed by the soldiers before the
entrance (why on earth would the army need a big rock in front
of a tomb to keep in the dead?) was rolled away. An angel, messenger of God, perched impudently upon the rock.

The angel preached the first Easter sermon: "Don't be afraid.
You seek Jesus, who was crucified? He is risen! Come, look at
where he once lay in the tomb." Then the angel commissioned
the women to become Jesus' first preachers: "Go, tell the men
that he has already gone back to Galilee. There you will meet
him."

It was a typically Jesus sort of moment, with people thinking
they were coming close to where Jesus was resting only to be told
to "Go!" somewhere else. Jesus is God in motion, on the road,
constantly going somewhere, often to where he is not invited.

Jesus was warned by his disciples not to go to Jerusalem. But Jesus, ever the bold traveler, did not let danger deter him, with predictable results—his death on a cross. And now, on the first Easter morning, death cannot daunt his mission. Jesus is once again on the move. So the angel says to the women, "You're looking for Jesus? Sorry, just missed him. By this time in the day, he's already in Galilee. If you are going to be with Jesus, you had better get moving!"

It's the week after Easter, time after resurrection. Let's get moving. (April 13, 2009)

THINKING RESURRECTION

Gerard Manley Hopkins has a poem in which he inserts the prayer, "Easter in us." He uses the noun *Easter* as a verb. "Easter in us." Let Easter get in to us, come where we live, permeate our souls. This sounds not only grammatically, but also theologically strange. Perhaps that's how the resurrection feels to us—as an active verb, not a passive noun.

Luke has a fast-paced account of the startling events of Easter. The women arrive at the tomb and in amazement discover he is not there, he has risen. Then Luke turns to what happens later in the day. "Now on that same day two of them were going to a village called Emmaus, . . . talking with each other about all these things that had happened. While they were talking and discussing, Jesus himself came near . . . but their eyes were kept from recognizing him" (24:13-16).

They didn't know Jesus. Two of his closest disciples didn't know him! It had only been three days since they had dinner with him. Now, on Sunday afternoon, they didn't know him.

Here is our question for today, class. Why didn't they know him? Luke says, "Their eyes were kept from recognizing him." Yes. But why?

Every now and then some sweet person will say something to me like, "I just don't get it. God has never spoken to me. When

I tried prayer, I was just talking to myself. This whole religion thing just seems like so much hooey." Perhaps their "I just don't get it" may be a testimonial not to lack of intelligence but rather to their possession of a particular kind of intelligence.

There is among us a sort of intelligence that has been wonderfully productive of all sorts of things: bridges, penicillin, fax machines, quantum physics, Britney Spears. And yet that same intelligence—so enamored with empiricism, facts and figures, and common sense—has its limits.

As Douglas Sloane, in his book on higher education, puts it, in American universities at least since the early 1900s quantifiable thinking (statistics, matter, money) has reigned supreme, while qualifiable thinking (thoughts of beauty, right and wrong, good and bad) has had a rough go of it.

Augustine, a bright young man with a superior classical education, confessed to Bishop Ambrose that he had tried to read the Bible but frankly, he was unimpressed. To him the Bible seemed like woefully inferior literature, crudely written, poorly edited. "You young fool," replied Ambrose. "You can't get it because when you read in the Bible about 'fish,' you think 'fish.' When you read 'bread,' you think 'bread.'" Ambrose explained to him the spiritual depth of Scripture, showing young Augustine levels of meaning beyond the surface appearance of things.

Thus later, after entering this strange new world of the Bible, Augustine sat under a tree in a garden. He heard a child singing, "Take up and read, take up and read." Was it the voice of a child or an angel? By this time his imagination was so excited, his consciousness so heightened that he couldn't tell the difference. He did what the voice said, took up the Bible, flopped it open to an obscure passage from Romans, and his life was changed forever. After that, we called him "St. Augustine."

This week I'm speaking at Wake Forest University. When I was a college chaplain I realized that the students with whom I worked were quite smart but were also those on whom we had spent years of education, and a fortune in tuition, beating into them the notion that the world is flat. A tree is a tree. A mystery is to be explained. A miracle is to be disproved. Everything going on out there is the result of some easily discovered material cause and everything going on in here is due to something your mother did to you when you were three. It's the modern world—closed, fixed, flat, demystified, disenchanted, and dull. Don't expect surprises and if by God's grace a surprise really occurs, don't expect to get it because you've lost the means even to know a surprise if you get one.

Why didn't they recognize Jesus when he walked along the road with them? We get defeated by the limited, officially sanctioned, governmentally subsidized world view. Death blinds us, tells us that the world is closed shut and if there is an intrusion, an invasion not of our own devising, we don't get it.

Two followers of Jesus are trudging along the dusty road seven miles from Jerusalem to Emmaus when suddenly the risen Christ joins them incognito on their journey. The risen Christ is to them a stranger. By the time they reach the end of their journey, they have moved from discouragement and despair to hope and faith. That's the road each of us (if Easter Sunday is half true to its promise) gets to walk.

The road to Emmaus is the way. That was the first name for the church—The Way. The church, when it is half true to its promise, is a group of people on a road where, wonder of wonders, the risen Christ meets us. If you want to experience the resurrection of Jesus Christ in your life, where you live, just get up in the morning and put one foot in front of the other and head down the road. Follow the way. But please, go with a bit of imagination. Walk with the expectation of the possibility of surprise.

John Dominic Crossan says that there are three different places in the Holy Land which claim to be the village of Emmaus. Three places! Furthermore, he says that there is no record of any village called "Emmaus" in any ancient source. The only place in all of the writings in the New Testament where we hear of the village of Emmaus is here in Luke's Gospel. Crossan says, "Emmaus is nowhere. Emmaus is everywhere."

As you are on the way, either at church or in a dormitory or at a family dinner table, Emmaus is wherever in your life journey

25

your eyes are opened by the grace of God and you see the risen Christ present. Easter in you. (April 7, 2008)

CHRIST GOT UP

We were just following the Order of Worship, going through the motions, and all so decently and in order, like every Sunday. But before we even had the Offering, Christ got up and left. Some overheard him mumble on the way out, "I'm sick of what you've done to Sunday. I'm doing Easter."

We were just having a meeting, plodding our way through the agenda, careful that all was in accord with *The Book of Discipline*, allowing everyone to have a say, taking every comment seriously, honoring proper process, when Christ got up and headed for the door. "This is boring," we heard him say on his way out.

We were just being church, exerting a positive influence on the community, just caring for one another, helping folks make it through the week, just affirming family values, instilling a positive attitude when Christ sighed, groaned, and got up and said, "I need some air."

We were just wilting, sagging, wearing down, wearing out, going limp, ready to throw in the towel, when Christ got up and, with a smirk, said, "I'm going to start a revolution. Anybody want to start a fire?"

We were just settling in, fluffing the pillows, getting comfortable, feeling safe with one another, accustomed to the surroundings, when Christ got up and screamed, "I'm the way! Truth! I'm the life! Follow me!"

We were just reading Scripture, extracting important biblical principles from the text, retrieving significant ideas for daily living, recovering basic fundamentals, noting historical precedents, when Christ got up and slammed the big book shut, saying, "Let's go do it rather than talk about it."

We were just sealing him safe and sound in the tomb, just making sure that the gravestone was in place, just getting adjusted to life without him, just obeying the soldiers, just accommodating ourselves to death and defeat when Christ got up, kicked the stone away, strode forth before our fearful faces, and ordered, "Get up!"

If we will go with him, I guess we've got to get up. Get up. (March 28, 2005)

THE PRACTICAL, ORGANIZATIONAL RELEVANCE OF RESURRECTION

In a workshop last year with an expert in church leadership, someone asked him, "You are a natural leader in starting new churches. What is the main thing you look for in selecting new pastors?" He responded, "An orthodox faith, a vivid belief in the Trinity, and of course, a sure faith in the resurrection."

Don't you find that an amazing response? I thought he would say something managerial, "an entrepreneurial spirit," something like that. Or, I thought he might cite some psychological configuration or organizational expertise in the pastor. No; it has to be theology, faith in resurrection.

It really makes a huge difference as we go about reaching a new generation of Christians, starting new churches, energizing established congregations, making disciples (our Conference priorities), if Jesus Christ has risen from the dead. If Easter is not true, then why bother?

Since Jesus Christ is raised, let loose, invading this world, returning to the very people who betrayed him, then we work not alone. The risen Christ goes before us. We serve a God who lives to raise the dead—even us. Therefore, we work with hope—not hope in ourselves and our efforts, but hope in Christ.

A couple of years ago, a District Superintendent paid me one of the greatest compliments I've ever received. He had told a pastor of our interest in moving him to a different church. "I can't do this," responded the pastor. "That church is dead. It's been dying for years and now I hear it's really dead." The DS replied, "I'll tell the Bishop, but let me warn you, this guy really believes that Easter is true. To tell him a pastor or a church is dead means nothing to him. He just sees death as an opportunity to see what Jesus can do." (March 23, 2008)

C H A P T E R   4

THE WORK OF THE CHURCH

EFFECTIVE CONGREGATIONS

Earlier this year our Conference Lay Leader, Ellen Harris, and I participated in a conversation with jurisdictional leaders on what makes for an effective congregation. What are some of the main characteristics of a growing, effective church? I thought they devised a fascinating list. How does your congregation embody, or conflict with, these characteristics?

Effective congregations:

1. Love their particular communities. Their pastors have found a way to love not only their congregations but also their neighborhoods. Effective pastors help their congregations move beyond love of themselves, turning their congregations outward.

2. Rise above mere contentment with things as they are and do what is necessary to expect and welcome change, disruption, and movement, similar to those of the risen Christ.

3. Find a way to welcome the stranger and practice radical hospitality in the name of Jesus Christ. They find

a way to be as interested in those who have yet to join the church as in those already in the church.

4. Have a clear sense of their primary purpose and keep focused on their primary God-given missions.

5. Enable lay leaders to lead, not just manage. The lay leadership feels a strong sense of responsibility for the future of its congregation.

6. All have a strong, change-oriented, gifted pastor.

7. Make growth a priority and figure out how to grow.

8. Keep focused upon Jesus Christ as the originator of and the purpose for the church (rather than church as just another human-oriented institution).

How does your church answer to these qualities of effective churches? What specific steps would your congregation need to take to live into the future in a different way? (December 8, 2008)

BEING HONEST ABOUT CHURCHES

Bill Easum has given his life to the renewal of congregations. Easum is one of our most creative and compelling proponents of church growth. He has enabled hundreds of congregations to reclaim their God-given ministry and to grow. I have found some of Easum's insights helpful in my work with the North Alabama Cabinet.

And yet, Easum admits that there are some rare exceptions to his rules for congregational development. He admits that some contexts do exist where no matter what a person does, nothing will change. Easum believes that clergy and congregational leaders ought to do all they can to grow a congregation, but that they ought not to be burdened with inappropriate guilt. Sometimes the most faithful thing is to admit that a congregation simply cannot grow and then to keep the congregation comfortable as it continues to experience inevitable decline.

Among those contexts that Easum says are examples of churches that will probably not grow:

1. Congregations located in areas from which most of the people have moved.
2. Congregations with a family system so dysfunctional that it would take the death of most of the leaders for the church to have a chance at new life. These churches are terminally ill and it is best to be honest about it.
3. Congregations that don't want to do anything but rot!
4. Congregations where almost all of the people are related to one another.

Sober words about honest assessment of congregational prospects from a proponent of growth. My goal is for every congregation in our Connection to be challenged with Jesus' call to grow. Yet if, for any of the above reasons, a church cannot grow, then I think we ought to admit it and move into a ministry of maintenance and care (which is always a prelude to eventual closure). Adequate support and supervision of all our churches, with only eight districts, is going to be a challenge for us. But a much greater challenge is to give churches *appropriate* support and supervision. If a church has no visible mission, if a church has, in effect, decided to decline and die rather than to grow, then we must be honest about that church's decision and respond accordingly.

Churches are born, they grow, they grow old, and they die. Yet some churches are sometimes reborn. The challenge is to be there with the right sort of leadership and encouragement that is appropriate to the true nature of that congregation. (May 8, 2006)

WHAT'S THE POINT OF WORSHIP?

During the season of Lent, for the next three weeks, I'll focus my messages on worship as the central art of church. Sometimes we hear questions like this about what happens in our churches in worship:

> Frankly, I just don't get much out of the Sunday morning thing. A lot of the time, I like the music, particularly when it's contemporary. But there is a lot that goes on Sunday morning that doesn't do much for me. Am I supposed to feel something? I would think that being a Christian is more than sitting and listening. It is also doing. What is the good of the praying and the singing and the sitting and listening?

What is the chief end of humanity? The proper answer from the Westminster Confession: The chief end of humanity is to glorify God and enjoy him forever.

The Christian faith is a matter of God's offer of love in Christ and our response to that love. We respond to God's love with our loving acts of service toward those in need in the church and in the world. And yet we respond to God's love not only by loving deeds of service to others, but also by simply doing the things we do for God because God is God and we are God's children. We are called not simply to obey God but also to glorify God. Above all, we are called to *enjoy* God. We are called to *worship*.

Love is not love if it is simply a matter of obeying rules, running errands, and performing duties. Some things we do just because we enjoy being in the presence of our loved one. So we sing songs, write poetry, dance, clap our hands, share food, or simply prop up our feet and do nothing but enjoy being with one another. In these purposeless moments of sheer enjoyment, we come very close to what love is all about.

If someone asked a Christian, "What's the purpose of your worship? Why do you gather on Sunday and sing songs, dress up, kneel, march in processions, clap your hands, shed tears, speak, eat, and listen?" we could only say, "Because we are in love."

The most serious, most delightful business of Christians, when you get down to it, is "to glorify God and to enjoy him forever." In other words, to worship. Whether we are glorifying and enjoying God in church with our music, sermons, baptisms, and prayers or doing so outside of church in our social concern, witnessing, and charity, it is all for one purpose: to glorify God and to enjoy him forever.

I can't put it better than one of the most "pointless" and wonderful of the psalms, the very last one:

Praise the LORD!
Praise God in his sanctuary;
   praise him in his mighty firmament!
Praise him for his mighty deeds;
   praise him according to his exceeding greatness!

Praise him with trumpet sound;
   praise him with lute and harp!
Praise him with tambourine and dance;
   praise him with strings and pipe!
Praise him with clanging cymbals;
   praise him with loud clashing cymbals!
Let everything that breathes praise the LORD!
Praise the LORD! (Psalm 150)

Here is the heart of Christians at worship: pure praise done in love for the sheer enjoyment of a Creator who first loved and is therefore beloved. (February 26, 2007)

WHO BUT THE CHURCH WILL TELL SUCH A TRUTH?

Here we are, deep in Lent, the Christian season of penitence and introspection, season of admission of sin and confession of our finitude. We are in a mess. We are not gods unto ourselves. We are sinners. In this upbeat, feel-good, progressive society, who but the poor old church will tell such truth about us?

Lent begins with Ash Wednesday. I hope that you celebrated this day in your church. When I was a college chaplain, I loved Ash Wednesday. I got a rather perverse joy in standing before some strapping nineteen-year-old, smearing ashes on his forehead, and proclaiming, "From dust you have come and to dust you shall return." Who but the church will tell such truth?

Last year I published *Thank God It's Friday: Encountering the Seven Last Words from the Cross* (Abingdon). I enjoyed so much the discussions about this book we had in dozens of our churches. How well I remember a man, in one of the discussions, saying, "It's kind of invigorating to be told the truth about me. I really do need saving. I really do need a Savior who saves sinners."

"The good news of Jesus Christ is a thing of great comfort," said C. S. Lewis. "But it doesn't begin in comfort. It begins in distress and despair and there's no way to get to the comfort by bypassing the despair." Have a happy Lent. (March 10, 2008)

CHAPTER 5

COURAGEOUS DISCIPLESHIP

MY NAME IS WILL, AND I AM ADDICTED

Years ago, we learned to deride those naive pietists who said, "The way to change the world is to save individual souls." We informed them that simply to change an individual's heart was no substitute for changing the social, systemic structures which held people captive.

Today we seem captivated, not by pietistic revivalism, but rather by the excesses of the vast American self-help industry— a huge network of gurus, weekend seminars, books, tapes, and advice-givers who urge us to self-actualize, let out the child within, learn to love ourselves, not beat up on ourselves, and shake off the worst of all human evils—codependency.

In her wickedly funny (and, at times, very perceptive) *I'm Dysfunctional, You're Dysfunctional* (Addison-Wesley, 1992), Wendy Kaminer grills the burgeoning self-help, codependency, twelve-step gurus. Today, just about everybody is codependent, and rather proud of it, too—quite willing to tell us all about it on *Oprah*. An estimated fifteen million of us attend a support group somewhere. Many of these groups actually help people, yet many are testimony to the sickness of a society that loves to be sick and loves to get well and loves even more to talk about ourselves.

Melody Beattie, best-selling author of *Codependent No More*, defines codependency as being affected by someone else's behavior and obsessed with controlling it. Her definition fits about 90 percent of the really effective pastors I know. "Hello, my name is Pastor Smith and I am addicted to trying to help people." In the hands of the self-help gurus like Beattie most of us are addicted, sick, hung up, abused, and "codependent." In fact, as Anne Wilson Schaef asserts in *Co-Dependence: Misunderstood— Mistreated*, "When we talk about the addictive process, we are talking about civilization as we know it." There, that covers just about everybody.

As the codependent therapists see the world, we're all basically good, yet we are the hapless victims of the abusive behavior of others. Of course, it's never our fault. Beattie says that guilt is the great abuser. "Guilt makes *everything* harder.... We need to forgive ourselves." To which Kaminer replies, "There's a name for people who lack guilt and shame: sociopaths. We ought to be grateful if guilt makes things like murder and moral corruption 'harder.'"

Yet in the self-help books and weekend marathon workshops, codependents are made to feel guilty that they feel guilt. Public confession is big in these groups. You become an instant expert in pain, addiction, and victimization in these programs by having the guts to stand in front of people whom you have never met and tell intimate details of your life. Some of this public cleansing sounds somewhat like Christian confession. Some of the testimonials of how one was previously addicted to drugs, to sex, or to overeating but is now cured because "I learned to love me" sounds vaguely like being reborn in Jesus.

But it is not.

Cloying positive messages that "I am loveable" or self-aggrandizing demands to "Look out for yourself for a change" are not the gospel. Indeed, although I am not at present victimized by depression, it is depressing to note how many church groups, counselors, and religious publishing houses have bought, hook, line, and sinker, into the codependency fad as if it were easily transposed into the Christian message.

The gospel is not in the business of producing victims. Christian conversion is not a journey deeper, ever deeper into yourself, relentlessly scanning your psyche, your needs, your desires, and your hurts. Not everything painful that happens to us in life renders us victims. (Popular codependency writer John Bradshaw has the nerve to compare adult children of alcoholics to Holocaust survivors.) The Poor Me victimization motif which infects much of this literature degrades our language and makes it increasingly difficult for us to talk about genuine cases of victimization by genuinely traumatic events. The facile adaptation of the twelve-step process pioneered by Alcoholics Anonymous in an attempt to apply it to every possible human malady and annoyance degrades the process. We now have smokers who have formed support groups to help them deal with the trauma they have experienced at the hands of nonsmokers. When everyone is a victim, nobody is a victim.

"Men are suffering right now—young men especially," says Robert Bly, a self-help guru who has been granted credibility by some Christians. Who is to blame for the sad shape of men? Bly blames it upon their mothers. The cure for disagreeable, abusive women, Bly says, is to "bust them in the mouth."[1]

I agree with Kaminer when she says that we must launch "a more critical, political perspective" on this self-help phenomenon, particularly in its use of the term "codependency." By "political" she means power. Some sort of power configuration is behind any attempt to help, even when it's self-help, especially when it is self-help. The politics behind the codependency movement are troubling; they focus exclusively upon the individual, consider all psychological problems to be inherently unjust, and make victims of just about everybody.

An odd view of the self emerges in most of this literature. A person is someone who looks out for number one, who deflects all criticism of the self that does not originate solely within the self, who has no other life project more interesting than the care and feeding of the self, and for whom the world is a threatening and evil place capable of rendering great harm to our essentially good selves.

Kaminer has a moving account of her observation of a group of Cambodian women refugees, all victims of rape, torture, and unspeakable horrors at the hands of the Khmer Rouge. Codependent literature invariably invites comparison of the overeating, inept parenting, or addictions people suffer with other human suffering. Kaminer found these Cambodian women to be a helpful "reality check." All suffering may be suffering but not all suffering is equal. Never did Kaminer hear these women swapping trauma stories, never did they indulge in attempts at the one-upmanship of pain. Rather, they enjoyed the life that was shared in the group. They went on picnics together, tried out makeup together. They worked on life beyond the horrors they had experienced, horrors which they had little desire to dwell upon. "How do you help each other?" a social worker asked them. "Sometimes, we tell jokes," they replied. "Of all the groups I attended," says Kaminer, these women were "the only ones that left me with a sense of hope."

I'll admit it. I really am dependent upon the congregations I've served. I really am dependent upon the grace of God for nearly everything worthwhile in my life. I'll admit, I'm not yet as dependent on God as I would like to be, but I'm trying.

Hello, my name is Will and I am a preacher, addicted to the need to ask, "This is all well and good, but is it the gospel?" (August 22, 2005)

KEEPING WORK IN ITS PLACE

George MacLeod, founder of the Iona Community of Scotland, said that he took the job of cleaning the community's toilets so "I will not be tempted to preach irrelevant sermons on 'the dignity of all labor.'"

I haven't preached many sermons on the subject of work.

When I do preach on work, I will tell the congregation that I believe that the fabled "Protestant work ethic" is a decidedly mixed inheritance for the church. Martin Luther attacked medieval monasticism by dignifying all work as divinely ordained. You don't have to become a nun to serve God. Even the lowest servant cleaning floors in the rich man's house mops to the glory of God. God did not simply create the world and quit. God keeps creating and invites us, in even the humblest work, to join in God's continuing creativity.

Luther's thought on work is not so much a glorification of our human work, but rather a celebration of the work of God. When Luther uses "vocation" he uses it to refer more to tasks like marriage and family than to jobs. Our vocation is not work but *worship*.

Some time ago, I saw a book for Christian students. It began, "How can you serve Christ on campus?" Answer: "First, by studying hard. You are called to be a student. You have gifts and graces from God for study. You are not studying just for yourself, but for what you can eventually give to others through your study. Now, study!" That sounds like "vocation."

Unfortunately, the "Protestant work ethic" tended to elevate even the meanest job to the status of divinely ordained. Thus, today when we say "vocation," we mostly mean "job."

Sometimes the "Protestant work ethic" defended the indefensible. If you're in a demeaning, degrading job, this line of thought suggests it is because God put you there; therefore, don't strive to better your condition. Such thinking was a powerful hindrance to revolutionary thought and action.

Today, most people can expect seven job changes in their lifetime. Many of these will be forced upon them by external economic factors. How can these multiple changes, forced upon the worker from the outside, be called aspects of divine vocation?

While Protestantism, in its attempt to honor all work as a vocation from God, may have contributed to some of the abuses of capitalism, the Christian and the Jewish faiths also bear within them a prophetic critique of work. In Genesis, the first book of the Bible, humanity is graciously invited by God to work. God creates a garden, then invites the woman and the man to tend the garden. Yet Genesis also admits that work, gracious gift of God, can be a curse when abused and used in sinful ways. Adam and Eve are cursed by hard work when they're kicked out of God's garden.

We have no record that Jesus ever worked or urged anyone else to do so. The "call" of Jesus appears to be a call to ordinary people like fishermen and tax collectors to leave their careers and to follow him on his travels about Galilee. Thus, while work may be a good gift of God, our present structures of work are not divinely ordained. Work, like any human endeavor—sex, money, art—may be tainted with human sin. For some, that sin will take the form of *idolatry*, in which we give to our jobs honor and energy that should be reserved for God.

I think that we pastors ought to be cautious about claiming too much for work. Most of work's rewards are most mundane. For one thing, most of our friends are somehow related to our work. One of the most dehumanizing aspects of unemployment is the loneliness of the unemployed.

Also, from a Christian perspective, your work has value because it contributes, not to your well-being, but to someone else's. As a mechanic said to me recently, "People need me more than they need a brain surgeon. When I put somebody's car back on the road, they're grateful and I'm happy." Work is a major way we discover our dependency on one another, our connectedness in a wide web of other people's work.

For another thing, most of us work for the mundane but utterly necessary need to earn a living. Our work puts bread on the table. Rather than debate which forms of work contribute to our personhood and which do not, we ought to focus on which work fairly compensates a worker and which work doesn't. We ought to admit that most of us work for pay. While we are working for pay, we can achieve many other noble human values. But none of those noble values should deter us from the most basic value that all ought to have work and that all ought to be justly compensated for their work. A fair, living wage is more to the point than our high-sounding theological platitudes.

We are right to seek meaningful work, since work is a major task given by God to humanity. We are right to criticize our present structures of work, expecting them to be sinful and in need of reform in various ways. Our work, suggests our faith, can be a source of great joy and also of much pain. Making a life is more significant than making a living. (February 5, 2007)

TRAVELING LIGHT

> After this the Lord appointed seventy others and sent them on ahead of him. . . . He said to them, ". . . Carry no purse, no bag, no sandals; . . ." (Luke 10:1-4)

How are you at packing? One of the tough aspects of taking a trip is deciding what to take and what not to take. A tennis racquet? A Bible? Extra pair of socks? After enough travel, one often learns to travel light. Over-stuffed suitcases, dragged from here to there, crammed with things that you probably will never need, make for difficult travel. Methodist preachers ought to be experts at how to pack!

When Jesus sent out his disciples he told them to travel light. He told them not to take a bag, a purse, or extra sandals. He did not want them to be overburdened with lots of useless baggage. He wanted them to be free to do the work that he called them to do, unburdened by needless care.

In my previous ministry with young adults I noted that they are on a journey that requires careful packing. I would tell them, "As you move into your new job, your new course of study, or your new relationships, you will want to take with you your cherished values, your sense of who you are, your gifts from God. But there is also much that you ought to leave behind. Any life transition requires that you let go of some old things in order that you might embrace new things. There are some people who carry around unnecessary baggage throughout their whole lives and pay a heavy personal price for their inability to travel light."

For disciples at any age, past hurts must be left so that there may be healing. Resentments, injustices, fears that characterized our lives in the past, must be cast aside. It will be tough to go forward unless you are able to decide what not to take with you.

Prayer focus: *Make a list of two or three things that you need to leave behind as you grow in the days ahead. List three things that you need to take with you. Ask God for the courage to travel light.* (August 8, 2005)

A WAY WHEN THERE IS NO WAY

I have set before you life and death, blessings and curses. Choose life so that you and your descendants may live, loving the LORD your God, obeying him, and holding fast to him. (Deut. 30:19-20)

One of the most moving books of the twentieth century was Viktor Frankl's *Man's Search for Meaning*. Viktor Frankl was a distinguished psychotherapist who was uprooted and put in a Nazi concentration camp. He was separated from his wife and family, as were many of his fellow prisoners. His was a bleak, despair-producing situation. Many of his fellow prisoners fell into complete despair in the camp. They had lost everything, had been stripped of their human dignity, treated like the lowest of animals by their cruel Nazi overlords.

Little wonder then that some prisoners simply sat down and died. Frankl noted the deaths of a number of prisoners who were not particularly ill or ill treated. They just simply stopped living. They saw themselves as utterly powerless, victims of cruel fate. With no way out, little hope of escape from the prison, they died. Their deaths were caused not only by the Nazis who put them into the camp but also by their own choices. They decided to quit.

Frankl took another way. Each day, while being marched out to the work site, he thought of a book that he had been writing. He composed the book in his mind, chapter by chapter. In his mind, he went back over the various aspects of the book. He thought of his wife. He pictured their good times in the past; he fantasized about the future they would have together. Thus Frankl survived. His survival was not only a miraculous act of

God, but also due to his own conscious efforts, his own choice to find meaning in this place of terrible meaninglessness.

Maybe our freedom to choose, our ability in every situation to decide, is one of God's greatest gifts to us. Perhaps we are not as trapped as we think. Even when there appears to be no way, there can be, by God's grace, a way.

Prayer focus: *Think about those areas of your life in which you feel caught, trapped, or out of control. Now bring those areas to God in prayer, asking God to help you to live courageously and boldly, to decide, and to choose to take charge.* (July 11, 2005)

NOTE

1. Robert Bly, *Iron John: A Book about Men* (Cambridge, Mass.: DaCapo Press, 2004), 100.

CHAPTER 6

THEOLOGICAL POLITICS

MIXING RELIGION AND POLITICS

A talk given to the Birmingham, Alabama Rotary.

Early Sunday morning, sitting in my office at Duke University Chapel, the phone rings. A nasal voice on the end asks, "Who's preaching in Duke Chapel this morning? I am trying to decide whether or not to drive over from Raleigh for the service." I clear my voice and say resonantly, "The Reverend Dr. William H. Willimon, Dean of the Chapel." The voice from Raleigh responds, "Good, I am coming over." I then ask, "Why is that good?" The voice responds, "I am a Baptist. I am so sick of hearing about nothing but politics in sermons. I've got to hear a sermon about Jesus."

I put down the phone and thought to myself, "How old am I?" When I was a young pastor, it was always we liberal, mainline pastors who were told, "Boy, you need to stick to saving souls and stay out of politics." Now, the roles have switched. It's mainly conservative, evangelical Christians who are more strongly mixing religion and politics. My, how things have changed.

Of course, mixing religion with politics is as old as our republic, and it remains one of the most distinctive aspects of

American democracy. And I am sure that when the story is told about the politics of the United States in the late twentieth century, the most interesting story will be the resurgence of evangelical political activism. I say "resurgence" because evangelicals mixing their religion with politics is nothing new.

Evangelical, Protestant Christians in the United States were extremely active in the nineteenth century, founding some of this country's most important colleges (we Methodists founded over three hundred of them), universities, hospitals, and orphanages. The Women's Christian Temperance Movement was the largest women's organization in the world, dedicating itself to personal transformation and political activism. It may still have the record of being the largest women's organization the world has ever known. American Jews were instrumental in the creation of and the continuing support for the state of Israel. Those of us in Alabama know that the civil rights movement was in great part a religious movement. When racist terrorists wanted to do damage to the movement for civil rights, they didn't bomb a Birmingham courthouse or post office; they bombed Birmingham churches. My own church, the United Methodist, has a three-story building on Capitol Hill, a block away from Congress, so that we can offer important advice to Congress and lobby them on issues Methodists feel are important.

Americans have always mixed religion with politics. And yet, this is not an easy mix, for reasons having to do with the nature of our politics and the nature of our religion. Thus, I have a three-point sermon for you.

1.

Religion is a continuing aspect of American political life. True, there was a time when Jimmy Carter had to say that even though he was a "born again" Baptist, if he were president, that wouldn't make a lot of difference. And you all remember the historic occasion when John Kennedy had to meet before the preachers in Texas and tell them that, even though he was a Catholic, he would pay more attention to Congress than to the pope.

If we are going to do politics the American way we have got to let all the people have their say, including us religious people. Editorials in the *New York Times* fulminate against narrow-minded religious bigots and fanatics. But in my experience, when you call someone a bigot and a fanatic, what you often mean is simply that their politics are different from yours.

I've got to be honest. I can't stand James Dobson, and I am chagrined that he has the ear of President Bush. But the main reason why is not because James Dobson is a "fanatic," it's just that he is wrong about both politics and religion (translated, that means that he has views different from mine!). James Dobson is no more "fanatic" or "closed-minded" than I am about my convictions; he is simply more effective!

2.

Politics is a risky business for religious people, particularly Christian people, who are the only religious people I know much about. Nobody goes to church primarily for politics. Nobody chooses a church simply because that church is politically to the right or to the left. People go to church to meet God, to have their lives exposed to the glare of God's judgments and grace. It is the nature of religious faith that whenever it is used for any other purpose, other than worship of and service to God, then that religion is being used and therefore abused. (This is a prejudiced Christian comment, the only kind you would expect me to make, but I find it sort of sad when religious people allow their religious convictions and their religious communities to be degraded by being used simply for certain political ends.)

Furthermore, I think we Christians need to be honest that when Christians get into politics, we are entering in many ways a very different world with different values and structures of authority. For instance, a friend of mine is an Islamic scholar. He casually remarked one day that the Koran, the holy book of Muslims, has absolutely no instructions for how Muslims are to behave when they find themselves a minority in a majority non-Muslim culture. If they find themselves in such a situation, they are to change the culture into a God-fearing (that is, Islamic) culture.

Of course, you knew what I was thinking when he said this. I realized that in our Christian Scriptures we have absolutely no instruction for how to behave when you have power, when you are in charge of things, when you are president of a bank or mayor of a town. All of our New Testament is distinctly minority literature, the literature of the powerless and the marginalized.

Jesus gave us a great deal of instruction on what to do after a divorce or what to do when someone slaps us on the right cheek, but no instruction on how to run a government. Jesus Christ was crucified by the greatest government the world had ever known, with the most noble system of laws that the world had ever known. Rome. That ought to teach us Christians to be very wary and suspicious when we encounter governments and their laws, even if they presume to be democratic.

In conversation with Jerry Falwell a number of years ago, I told Mr. Falwell that my main objection to him was that he acted like a "Methodist from the 1950s." I reminded him that it was liberal mainline Christians like me who said in the 1950s, "Oh, if we can just get an invitation to the White House. Oh, if we could just get a few more Senators elected who have Christian principles in their souls." It has been years since I've heard Methodists talk like that. Now the only people talking like that are the people who follow Jerry Falwell.

When I met with United Methodist legislators in Montgomery to ask them how I could help them better fulfill their ministry in public service, one of the things they told me was this: "Bishop, please do everything you can to let the citizens of Alabama know that there is more than one Christian view on most political subjects. To be a Christian is to be part of a dizzying variety of theologies and perspectives on just about anything. Please let people know that there is no one, single Christian view on highway construction."

It is the nature of the Christian faith to be rather messy, to include a variety of voices and perspectives. So that means that when you ask Christians, "What do you think we ought to do on this particular political issue?" you are going to hear a variety of

voices, and no one voice can lay claim to being the one authori-
tative, uncontested Christian voice.

3.

And my third point is that when we religious folk play the
political game, we must play through political rules. Politics fol-
lows a different set of rules, rules that apply in a non-religious,
secular, constitutional democracy. (I don't really believe there is
much biblical support for democracy, though democracy has been
a good system of government for us Christians. In the Bible, it's
all hierarchy, God's authority that overrules everybody else, and
there is no place for majority vote—truth determined by who can
get the most votes. Our truth comes from God, or so we believe.)

It is not fair for Christians to get into politics and then try to
exclude other voices. Politics is the art of compromise, but most
religious faiths consider compromise to be a bad thing. I am troubled when Christians attempt to force through legislation some
standards we can't even achieve in our own churches.

How well I remember sitting in a church meeting a number of
years ago in which we were drafting a letter to our state legisla-
ture demanding the requirement of access to all persons with
physical disabilities in all buildings in our state. A woman who
had a daughter confined to a wheelchair rose and said, "You hyp-
ocrites! How many of you serve churches that are totally accessible to handicapped persons? How many of you have made sure
that your churches are completely welcoming and accessible? It is
always easier to spend somebody else's tax money to work justice
than to do justice right in your own churches." I thought she had
a point.

If I think the Christian faith is against abortion, and it certainly seems to me that it is, my first task is to convert and convince folk in my congregations of that before I work on the rest
of you who don't believe what I believe about the world, including who is in charge of the world (that is, Jesus). I think the best
way that we churches can have a political voice is to be examples
of something that the world is not—a countercommunity (the

church) that is different from that which can be achieved through politics.

Again, another prejudiced Christian statement, but I must say, after returning from working in Mississippi last week with three hundred United Methodist preachers, if you have a hurricane blow through your town, totally destroy your life, and make you want to kill yourself because you've lost everything, you will be a lot better served by Christian people than you will be served by FEMA or the Red Cross! The government has a way of killing so many things that it touches. There are things that we've allowed the government to do that people of faith can do better.

One day Jesus was walking along and he was asked a political question. "Jesus, should we pay taxes to Caesar or not?" (Note that Jesus, who appears to be utterly nonchalant, disinterested in politics, did not raise the question of the coin; it was our question.) You know what Jesus did in response to this perfectly clear political question? He asked, "Who has a coin?" (His pockets were empty.) "Whose picture is on the coin?" "Caesar's." "Well, it's kind of sad that he needs to put his picture all over money in order to feel better about himself, but go ahead and give it to Caesar since it appears to be his. But you be careful, don't you dare give to Caesar what belongs to God." And then Jesus proceeded along on his journey.

Could I note just a few things here? First of all, this is our question, not Jesus'. Why do we think politics is so important in the first place? Why has politics become the major source of meaning and significance in our lives, the solution to every problem?

Point two, note that Jesus' pockets are empty. He seems to be practicing a life of very different "politics" from ours. When politics gets degraded—away from the search for the common good—and becomes a greedy matter of how much money you can keep in my pocket for me, or how we can structure our government to benefit a few, it just may be that politics is something which Jesus has no interest in.

Three, notice that Jesus, when asked about politics, considers it *a matter of worship*. Whose image do you bow before? What would you sacrifice your children for? What is most important to you? Politics and idolatry are here linked by Jesus.

Four, note that Jesus really doesn't answer the question. He doesn't really define what Caesar owns and what God owns. That means that when it comes to politics, maybe the Christian point of view is to be permanently uneasy, never quite sure, when we're giving to Caesar what really ought to belong to God.

This says to me that if Christians are going to get in bed with Caesar, if we are going to be deeply involved in politics, we ought to be tossing and turning all night, the most nervous and uneasy of bedfellows! (October 24, 2005)

THINKING LIKE A CHRISTIAN

In his fine new book, *Methodism: Empire of the Spirit,* historian David Hempton shows that part of the genius of early Methodism was its ability to hold together seemingly contradictory ideas in its mind at one time. Against Calvinistic reductionism, we held together the universal salvation wrought by Christ *and* the need for a personal, life-changing commitment by each person. Against Lutheran reductionism, we held together justification *and* sanctification. Against Puritan anti-sacramentalism, we held together preaching *and* sacraments, the local congregation and the holy catholic church, free church *and* catholic forms of worship.

Thomas Langford, in his wonderful book *Wesleyan Theology,* said that Methodism was never tempted by simplistic fundamentalism because of our high doctrine of the Holy Spirit. This, said Langford, preserved us from one-sided theological affirmations and myopic fanaticism while at the same time imbuing our movement with a passion for winning souls *and* serving the needs of the world.

Today I fear that "single-issue politics" are impoverishing our political life and single-issue thinking is threatening our Methodist way of serving Christ. One of the things wrong with

51

the "Hearts on Fire!" meeting that met recently at Junaluska was that these sisters and brothers have seized upon one issue of the faith, have climbed up on some self-presumed moral high ground, and have pushed this to the virtual exclusion of larger concerns about the church and the church's mission today.

One of the things wrong with their self-righteous critics like Donald Wildman and the Institute on Religion and Democracy (IRD) is that they have seized upon that same issue as *the* test of our faith, climbed up on high moral ground, and drawn a line in the sand to the virtual exclusion of other body of Christ concerns. Having had hundreds of emails from both groups, having been vilified by the Reconciling movement and praised by the IRD, I can hardly tell the difference between the two. They both have reduced the bubbling, living, exuberant Christian faith to one issue. They both are so firmly convinced that their position is the biblical, righteous position and their opponents are utterly wrong. I would urge our United Methodists not to let these fringe groups determine the mission of our church. Christ has given us our mission and that mission is considerably more demanding, complex, and exciting than these little groups admit.

It is so hard to think with the expansiveness that is demanded by a God who is fully human *and* fully divine, completely gracious *and* scathingly judgmental, wonderfully accepting *and* extravagantly demanding. I know why there are Muslim "fundamentalists," for I have tried to read through the Koran, the holy book of Islam. I am not surprised that the style of the Koran tends to produce a kind of monism. But for the life of me—as someone who works on a weekly basis with the living, elusive, peripatetic Christ and the Trinitarian God who is rendered in the complexity of Holy Scripture—I can't figure out Christian fundamentalists. Those in our church who jump on one issue as *the* one, absolutely essential, undeniable test of fidelity to Jesus seem perilously close to fundamentalism.

Let's keep pushing one another to thinking that is worthy of the gospel and as fully faithful to the full gospel as possible. I'm not asking for tolerance, for broad-mindedness, or some other limp, liberal, secular virtue. I'm talking about thinking that's as thick and complex as Jesus. (September 19, 2005)

THINKING LIKE A CHRISTIAN 2

I've just returned from the third of our "Bishop's Conversations on the Iraq War." Thanks to Anne Wheeler and her team for organizing these events. Nearly four hundred Alabama United Methodists engaged in fruitful, prayerful conversation and thereby modeled Wesleyan "Christian Conferencing." These conversations were planned to be learning experiences. I told each group, "Here we are going to try to think like Christians about war and this war. We will try to think biblically and in a specifically Christian way."

I was proud of the way we discussed a passionate, controversial issue. I hope that everyone present grew in faith and understanding. I sure did. Here are some of my learnings:

1. It's a real challenge to think about things as *followers of Jesus Christ*. It's much easier to think like Americans of the left or of the right, to ask merely, "What works?" or "What do most people think?" It's a challenge to ask, "What does Jesus require of his followers?" or "What does the Bible say?"

2. There is no Christian consensus on the current war, even though I did find general agreement that Scripture and the church's tradition make war, this war in particular, or any other war, a questionable action for Christians. Christians who defend war as an appropriate response to evil and conflict have got their work cut out for them.

3. Those United Methodists who defend the war as justifiable are diverse and conflicted in what they think about the war. Many people who believe this war is justified believe that those who initiated it have done a

terrible job of executing it. There are many diverse opinions, which is one reason why I don't think "resolutions"
do justice to the complexity of the issue.

4. There is widespread regret and even deep repen-
tance among our United Methodist people about this
war.

5. Many of our people are eager for their pastors and
their church to give them help in thinking like
Christians about the war. They were grateful that their
church had these gatherings, though many felt that such
discussion was long overdue.

6. Church resolutions and statements by bishops or
Annual Conferences about this war may not be as help-
ful as prayerful, humble conversation with fellow
Christians. (Perhaps I was the one who said that!)
(September 1, 2008)

JESUS THE IMMIGRANT

We're in the Sundays after Epiphany, that time after
Christmas. What did Jesus and the Holy Family do right after
Christmas? They became refugees, immigrating to Egypt, fleeing
an oppressive government at home. If Egypt, for all of its pagan
limits, had not received Jesus, Mary, and Joseph and protected
them, then our salvation would have been jeopardized. That's
why Christians have a peculiar slant on issues of immigration.
We know the story of Jesus the refugee. Our Lord has commanded us to receive the sojourner, the alien within our gates,
remembering that all of us were alienated from God until Jesus
showed us hospitality.

Among Alabama United Methodists, we have had some of our
most astounding evangelistic success among Spanish-speaking
persons. These sisters and brothers found not only the United
States but also Methodism. The recipient of this year's Denman
Evangelism award is one of our Spanish-speaking pastors who is

being unfairly harassed by the INS, costing us much in church dollars to keep him working for Jesus in the U.S.

Alas, some politicians are attempting to make political hay by making life more difficult for the newest Americans by linking fear of immigration with fear of terrorism. In December the House of Representatives passed HR 4437, the Border Protection, Antiterrorism, and Illegal Immigration Control Act of 2005, despite the opposition of many churches. The bill is now in the Senate and may be considered by the Judiciary committee as early as March 2. It looks to me like this bill is not only mean-spirited but also fails to address comprehensive immigration reform. It doesn't include any provision for a guest worker program, an earned legalization program, or a reduction in the backlogs for family-based immigration. Instead, the bill criminalizes undocumented people for unlawful presence in the United States, including those who work or volunteer with faith-based organizations like ours.

Personally, I like the Secure America and Orderly Immigration Act (S.1033), introduced by Senators McCain (R-AZ) and Kennedy (D-MA). I have found helpful information at the faith-based website: http://www.justiceforimmigrants.org/action.html. I urge all of you, as followers of Jesus Christ, the Immigrant, to examine this legislation, let your representatives know how you feel, and prayerfully consider how best to show Christian hospitality in your churches to our fellow immigrants. (February 15, 2006)

PATRIOTIC THOUGHTS

The other day, a letter caught my eye in *Christianity Today*:

I am a U.S. Army chaplain, have served a tour in Iraq, and proudly wear the uniform of my beloved country. Yet I have never felt comfortable participating in "Patriotic Sunday" services around the Fourth of July. The mixing of the symbols of God and country always remind me of the frightening photographs of German clergy proudly displaying the swastika in their churches and rendering the Nazi salute during the Third Reich. I have always wanted to avoid even the appearance of such a diabolical marriage of church and state in the United States.

During Sunday worship the week before Independence Day, I became convinced that such patriotic displays during the worship hour are nothing less than idolatry, i.e., the praise and adoration of something other than almighty God. Thank you for having the courage and insight to speak a prophetic word to the evangelical community at a time when our faith and our political persuasions are again being inappropriately commingled. Scott A. Sterling—Columbia, South Carolina[1]

I don't know Chaplain Sterling, though I have done much work among Army chaplains, including those at Fort Jackson. I do see this as a helpful reminder that the purpose of Sunday morning worship is the worship of the God of Israel and the church, the God of the Bible, the Prince of Peace, not the patron of America. We have our hands full on Sunday morning standing before and walking behind the cross—the flag is for other settings.

An Alabama layperson told me of visiting a service at a United Methodist church in Montgomery when our nation invaded Iraq. He complained that there were army insignia, flags, and an unabashed display of patriotic fervor. His little daughter left church that morning asking, "Dad, what did any of that have to do with Jesus?" While I hope that this wouldn't happen in a church in our Conference, still, I think it worth mentioning.

On the week of the war, *Good News* magazine, for which I have written, and which is supposed to be a "forum for scriptural Christianity," had a shameless flag-waving, government-praising issue which uncritically and unquestioningly (and I must say, unbiblically) supported the war. We're a long way from July Fourth, but I thought I might mention this now as a reminder that, as Christians, we're always struggling to worship the true God and to align our lives along the true path. As followers of Jesus, we are primarily citizens of the kingdom of God and secondarily citizens of a secular state. Our salvation is in the cross, rather than the flag. One of the best services we can render to our nation is the constant reiteration that God, not nations, rules the world. Thanks to Chaplain Sterling for reminding me of this. (September 12, 2005)

A PRAYER FOR GEORGE ALEXANDER, JR.

Lord Jesus, King of Kings, Savior of the World, Prince of Peace, hear this prayer for George, son of Alabama, two-thousandth American soldier to die in our war in Iraq. Receive him, we pray—a lamb of Your flock, a sinner for whom You have died, a cherished and beloved child of God—and one who is at peace at last, because he is with You.

George had an Alabama boyhood, an Alabama youth, and Alabama dreams. I pray for his mother, his family and friends, his church, and all those for whom his death means not only the ending of his dreams, but the beginning of their lifetime of grief and loss. Lord, help us to feel some measure of their pain. Save us from offering cheap consolation or patriotic platitudes in the face of their loss. Instill in our hard hearts a determination to work with You for a government in which we shall make peace as quickly and resourcefully as we make war, a country that loves Your righteousness and justice more than our security and power.

One and Only Way, Truth, and Life, give us the grace to live by Your word rather than by our weapons. Lord Jesus, You never lifted Your hand against anyone, You refused to defend Yourself even when unjustly attacked, You resisted violence with peace and nonviolence, and You never, ever told us that war was the answer to anything. When will we move from worshiping You to following You?

Seeker and Lover of the Lost, forgive us of our sin of attempting to solve the world's problems through violence and war. Forgive us of our willingness to once again allow old people like me to send young people like George to make war on others and to suffer and die to preserve our privileges. Forgive us for loving our freedom more than Your peace, and for treating Your gift of life so casually. Give us, in our grief for our fallen daughters and sons, an equal amount of grief for the deaths of the twenty-five thousand Iraqi sisters and brothers in Christ. Grant us a miracle: that George may be not only the two-thousandth young American to die in this war, but also the last.

Judge of us all, I confess that I have not prayed enough, have not embodied Your truth enough, have not been critical enough of our political leaders, have acquiesced to the plans of the initiators and makers of war, rather than joining the ranks of Your blessed makers of peace. In Your name, and in heartfelt grief for the loss of George, and in bold confidence in Your coming kingdom, I pray.

Amen. (October 27, 2005)

NOTE

1. *Christianity Today* (September 2005): 17.

CHAPTER 7

WOMEN AND MINISTRY

DIVINE WISDOM AMONG "LITTLE OLD LADIES"

A few years ago a friend of mine returned from one of those National Council of Churches trips to the former Soviet Union. Two weeks had made her a Soviet expert. When asked about the churches in there, her reply was, "There's nobody left in the churches except for a few little old ladies." Poor, out-of-it church. Nobody left but a few little old ladies.

In light of the complete collapse of the Soviet Union and the resurgence of the church in Russia and the former Soviet Republics, we are now better able to assess the relative importance of those few believing women. As it turned out, those women had put down their money on the right horse. While leaders of the World Council of Churches were busy having dialogue with the Communist bosses in Romania and elsewhere (the very same bosses who were making life so miserable for Christians there), the pastor of a little Romanian Reformed church, probably assisted by a few "little old ladies," was busy bringing down an empire. And as usual, no one was more surprised by all this than those of us in the church.

When will we ever learn the truth that God has chosen "what is foolish in the world to shame the wise; God chose what is weak in the world to shame the strong; God chose what is low and despised in the world, things that are not, to reduce to nothing things that are" (1 Cor. 1:27-28)? I know that this passage concludes with "so that no one might boast in the presence of God," but is it OK to boast in the presence of our half-hearted church that those believing women, that faithful pastor knew a great deal more about the way the world works than all of the Pentagon strategists, White House–Kremlin planners, World Council of Churches dialoguers, and most of the rest of us?

At the World Methodist Conference a few summers ago, the former dean of Duke Divinity School was talking with a bishop from one of the Baltic republics. "How in the world were you able to keep going with so many years of hostility and persecution?" he asked the bishop. "Well, though it was tough, we in the church always took the long view," was his reply.

Several years ago the World Methodist Council gave Mr. Gorbachev its "Peacemaker of the Year" award. A couple of months later, he ordered the tanks into Lithuania. As far as I know, he did not return the award.

Is it possible for us to look behind the encouraging headlines coming out of the East, to take the long view, to read them *sub specie aeternitatis* (from an eternal perspective), to let ourselves be schooled by those wise, so worldly wise, little old ladies who knew something that even the CIA did not?

I quickly learned, in my first parish, that if I really wanted something done, something pushy, a bit risky, something out of the ordinary, I needed to go to the members of the Alice Davis Memorial Circle of the United Methodist Women. It wasn't that they were all over seventy and had time, it was that they were all well formed as Christians and had faith. While Nixon was pondering whether or not to go to China, they were finishing the UMW Fall Mission Study on The People's Republic. When we all celebrated the end of the Vietnam War, they were sending letters to the people of Vietnam apologizing for our destruction of their country and putting aside a portion of their Social

Security checks to contribute to the Church World Service Refugee resettlement program. When I spoke to the church about the need to do something about the plight of the homeless, three of them came forward to tell me that they work as volunteers at the homeless shelter so, if I were really serious, they would be happy to take me for a visit.

Sometimes, there is nobody left to be the church "except for a few little old ladies." Thank God. (January 22, 2007)

THE REVEREND GRANDMA

My wife Patsy's grandmother was the first ordained woman in South Carolina Methodism. Since 1956, the Reverend Bessie B. Parker set a high standard of Christian ministry. This year we will celebrate the fiftieth anniversary of the ordination of women in our church. We'll be having a number of events, including a special emphasis at this year's Annual Conference. As a prelude to these celebrations, I offer this piece that I wrote for Christian Ministry *a few years ago celebrating the gift of Bessie Parker.*

According to Carlyle Marney, God will use any handle to get hold of somebody. Divine persistence and resourcefulness are, according to Scripture, virtually without limits. Bessie Parker was the handle God used to take hold of South Carolina for more than three decades until her death a few years ago. Bessie, who became a pastor in 1956, wore out automobiles the way her Methodist circuit-riding ancestors went through horses, routinely driving thirty thousand miles every year. Although she had a reputation for being one of the most effective preachers in the South Carolina Conference of The United Methodist Church, she was the bane of the bishops. Churches complained when they heard that they were getting a lady preacher, and they resisted even more obstinately four years later when the bishop dared to move our dear Reverend Parker somewhere else.

With snow-white hair and a soothing southern drawl, she epit-
omized everyone's stereotype of a grandmother. This she used for
everything it was worth. Preachers stood in line to enlist Bessie
to lead their annual mission-fund appeals. When she got to
preaching, telling congregants how much they were going to
enjoy sending breeder pigs down to Haiti (they will go down
there and make more piggies in the name of the Lord, Bessie
would giggle), pigs started packing. When one church repeatedly
refused to fix its leaking church roof, the members were scandal-
ized one Monday morning by the sight of their pastor (white hair,
blue jeans, and all) atop the roof, hammering away. The roof was
quickly repaired with everyone's willing assistance. It just doesn't
look right to have your grandmother up fixing the roof, one
church officer commented.

Toward the end of Bessie's ministry the bishop sent her to a
very difficult church, one infamous for feuding, contentiousness,
racism, and animosity toward the denomination. Before Bessie
arrived, the church had run off two preachers in six months.
Members had consistently refused to send any money to support
denominational programs. The bishop seemed cruel to send Bessie
there just before her retirement. Everyone predicted disaster.

A few months passed without my hearing a word about Bessie.
Then I saw her at a denominational meeting and, fearing the
worst, asked her how she was getting along at her new appoint-
ment. "The sweetest people I have ever known!" she exclaimed.
"Our first work team will leave for Brazil next month. I've got to
get back early: this is our music weekend with the neighboring
African American congregation."

I was dumbfounded. Were we talking about the same church?
What about its hatefulness? Its racism? Had there been no problems? "Not really," replied Bessie. "There was one little misunderstanding when we voted on this year's budget."
Misunderstanding? "Yes. We got to the apportionment for the
Black College Fund. When we were about to vote on acceptance,
the chairman of our board said, 'Reverend Parker, we don't give
no money to that because we ain't paying for no n*****s to go to
college.'"

"Oh no! What did you do?" I asked.

"I stood up and said, 'John, that's not nice. You sit down and act like a Christian.'" Everything passed without a single problem. Who's going to misbehave in front of his grandmother?

Richard Baxter advised seventeenth-century Protestant pastors that the tenderest love of a mother should not surpass ours for our people. Bessie routinely mothered the people toward the kingdom, using any handle she could to get across the gospel—just as God used Bessie. Thank God. (April 24, 2006)

A FAITH THAT IS BASED ON THE TESTIMONY OF WOMEN

When women went to the tomb in darkness on the first Easter morning, they were disheartened by the thought of a large stone placed by the soldiers before the entrance of the tomb. To their surprise, the stone was rolled away. An angel, a messenger of God, was perched impudently upon the rock.

The angel preached the first Easter sermon: "Don't be afraid. You seek Jesus, who was crucified? He is risen! Come, look at where he once lay in the tomb." Then the angel commissioned the women to become Jesus' first preachers: "Go, tell the men that he has already gone back to Galilee. There you will meet him." (How sad that there are still churches that continue, despite this clear witness of Scripture, to deny the testimony of women and to prohibit them from preaching the gospel that God has given to them—but I digress.)

The women obeyed and sure enough out in Galilee the risen Christ encountered them. Why Galilee? Though all of Jesus' disciples came from there, Galilee is in the Judean outback, a dusty, rural sort of place. Jesus himself hailed from Galilee, from Nazareth, a cheerless town in a forlorn region. ("Can anything good come out of Nazareth?" asked Nathaniel, before he met Jesus—John 1:46a.) Galilee was held in contempt by most Judeans. It was a notorious hotbed of Jewish resistance to Roman rule. So the risen Christ has returned, once again, to those who had so miserably forsaken and disappointed Jesus the first time around.

It's emblematic of Jesus. Despite his disciples' betrayal, the first day of his resurrected life, there's Jesus, risen from the dead, with nothing more pressing than rapidly to return to the rag-tag group of Galilean losers who had the first time so failed him.

And what does Jesus say to them? His last words, at least as Matthew remembers, are—"You have all had a rough time lately. Settle down and snuggle here in Galilee. After all, these are the good country folk with whom you are the most comfortable. Buy some real estate, build a church, and enjoy one another's company in a sort of spiritual club." No! The risen Christ commands, "Go! Get out of here! Make me disciples, baptizing and teaching everything I've commanded you! And don't limit yourselves to Judea. Go to everybody. I'll stick with you until the end of time just to be sure you obey me."

How like Jesus not to allow his people rest and peace, not to encourage them to hunker down with their own kind, but rather to send forth on the most perilous of missions those who had so disappointed him. They were, in Jesus' name, to go, to take back the world that belonged to God. Here we encounter an implication of Jesus' peripatetic nature: there is no way to be with Jesus, to love Jesus, without obeying Jesus, venturing with Jesus to "Go! Make disciples!"

By the way, in that time and in that place, the testimony of women was suspect, inadmissible in a court of law, ridiculed as being worthless. So why would the early church have staked everything on the testimony of these women at the tomb? You can be sure that if the men (hunkered down back in Jerusalem, I remind you) could have told the story of Jesus' resurrection another way they would have—unless it happened exactly that way.

Let's give thanks that these first preachers, these first evangelists, despite any fears they may have felt, despite any resistance they encountered from the men, stood up and told the truth of what they had seen and heard. Happy Easter! (April 20, 2009)

EVANGELISM, CONSUMERISM, AND THE EMERGING GENERATION

EVANGELISM AS THE INVITATION TO BE DIFFERENT

When I was in seminary, I got the impression that my job as a pastor was to help lessen the gap between the Bible and the "modern world." Here was the Bible, mired in the first century. Here was the skeptical, critical modern world. The pastor, through preaching and various acts of pastoral ministry, labored to lessen the gap, to bring the gospel close to where modern Americans lived.

Since then I have come to the conclusion that today's faithful pastor ought to clarify, even accentuate the gap between the Bible and the modern world rather than lessen the gap. Evangelism calls people, not to agreement, but to conversion, detoxification, the adoption of practices meant to save them from the deceits of the "modern world." In churches which have for so long called people to adjustment, we are calling for pastors willing to call people to alienation, to be, as in the title of a book by Hauerwas and me, *Resident Aliens*.[1]

I consider it a happy gift of God that here, at the beginning of the twenty-first century, increasing numbers of Christians in North America sense that something is wrong; they feel lost, cast adrift, afloat on a sea of uncertainty, homeless. Undoubtedly, the 1 Peter designation of early Christians as "aliens" and sojourners arose in a situation in which baptism pushed one to the periphery of the dominant order, not so much on the basis of baptism's demands, but rather because the dominant order is intolerant of anyone who fails to bow before the altar inscribed with the claim that all intolerance must be rejected except for the intolerance which says that we must be equally tolerant of all claims.

A few years ago when I was in Australia, where something less than 20 percent of the population is identified as Christian, there was a news story about a Pentecostal church in Sydney which had been vandalized for the second time in a month. Earlier, someone had started a fire at the church. Now, someone had shoved a fire hose in the window of the church, ruining the contents of the building. The church was located in a small business center so, when the vandals flooded the church, they also flooded the surrounding businesses.

The owner of a florist shop next door to the church complained, "No one told me, when I rented this shop, that I would be next door to a church. I'm really quite upset with having to have a business next to a church." The reporter asked a police spokesperson, "Do you think this is anti-religious violence here?" "Anti-religious? No. This was a church," said the policeman.

What impressed us was that, if these acts had been perpetrated against a mosque or a synagogue, *everyone* would have called it racist or anti-religious, for these groups are clearly at odds with the dominant order and are periodically attacked for that reason. There is as yet a failure to recognize that churches are increasingly finding themselves in exactly the same situation as our neighborhood mosque.

We live in wonderful times. The Christian faith has always done quite well during times of cultural chaos and the complete disintegration of society (otherwise known as downtown Birmingham). Baptism encourages us to embrace a new culture and community (church) which helps us to enjoy being weird.

Christians are not first called to be aliens. Jesus calls us to be *witnesses* "in Jerusalem, in all Judea and Samaria, and to the ends of the earth" (Acts 1:8). It is interesting that the Greek word for "witness" is the same root as our word *martyr*. Jesus has not called us to hunker down behind the barricades, but rather to "Go...and make disciples of all nations, baptizing them...teaching them..." (Matt. 28:19-20).

Yet it is important for the church as witness to have something to say which is more interesting than what the world says. Give the world credit, one reason why the world mostly ignores us is that we have so little to say that the world cannot hear elsewhere. When church becomes Rotary, church will lose, because Rotary serves lunch and meets at a convenient hour of the week!

The church exists not for itself, but rather to save the world, to "proclaim the mighty acts of him who called you out of darkness into his marvelous light" (1 Peter 2:9). So the question is not *if* we shall live as Christians in this world, for that is no option for us. Rather, the question is, now that God has entered this world as Jesus the Christ, *how* then shall we live?

One of my students came under the influence of a sect that was rumored to be working on campus. His parents called me, frantic to rescue him from the dominance of this demanding, separatist group. The group was completely monopolizing the young man's life. When I finally met with him, we talked about his experience with the group. When I asked, he told me that he had grown up in a Lutheran church in the Midwest and that his parents had been active in the church all their lives.

"Then why on earth, I must ask, could you become involved in this strange, fringe group?" I asked. "Well, it all started on the first Sunday I visited them. When I walked into their church, I saw black people, white people, people of every shade of the rainbow. You could feel the love. Our church had always *preached* this sort of loving fellowship to me. But I had never seen it until I walked into that group. I said to myself, 'This is the church I've always heard about but have never seen until now.'"

I waited some time before I asked him other questions. (November 28, 2005)

CHURCH OF THE SECOND CHANCE

In Anne Tyler's novel *Saint Maybe*, nineteen-year-old Ian tells his parents, Doug and Bee Bedloe, of his decision to leave college and become an apprentice cabinetmaker. This will enable Ian to raise the young children of his deceased brother, Danny. Ian has arrived at this decision because of the influence in his life of Rev. Emmett and the Church of the Second Chance, a congregation that believes in actual atonement, that is, that you must do something "real" to be forgiven for your sins. Ian's sin was that he led his drunken brother to believe that his wife was unfaithful, after which Danny committed suicide.

In the crucial scene in which Ian tells his parents of the change in the course of his life, church and faith enter the conversation. Ian explains that he will have help from his church in juggling his new job and the responsibility for the children. This alarms his parents.

"Ian, have you fallen into the hands of some sect?" his father asks. "No, I haven't," Ian says. "I have merely discovered a church that makes sense to me, the same as Dober Street Presbyterian makes sense to you and Mom." "Dober Street didn't ask us to abandon our educations," his mother tells him. "Of course we have nothing against religion; we raised all of you children to be Christians. But our church never asked us to abandon our entire way of life."

"Well, maybe it should have," Ian says.

His parents look at each other. His mother says, "I don't believe this. I do not believe it. No matter how long I've been a mother, it seems my children can still come up with something new and unexpected to do to me."[2]

Ian's is a story of two kinds of churches. Dober Street is a church that mainly confirms people's lives as they are. The Church of the Second Chance disrupts lives in the name of Jesus so that people can change. In my experience, young adults are more attracted to the church that promises them change, new life, and disruption than to the church that offers little but stability, order, and accommodation. Alas, too many of our churches have contented themselves with meeting the spiritual needs of one generation with the resulting loss of at least two generations of Christians. If we are going to fulfill our Conference priority and summon a new generation of young Christians, I expect that we'll have to look more like the Church of the Second Chance. (November 17, 2008)

THE CHURCH AND THE CONVERSION OF EMERGING ADULTS

One of our Conference priorities is to reach a new generation of Christians. Our focus is upon the eighteen-to-thirty age group, those who are being called "emerging adults." If we are to reach this age group—the age group that we have sadly neglected and therefore find absent from our churches—we are going to have to understand them. Fortunately, a number of new books are helpful in that regard.

A major defining characteristic of this age group is their postponement of marriage. In just a couple of decades the average age for women to marry moved from twenty to twenty-five years old, and then the average age for men rose from twenty-two to twenty-seven years old. Interestingly, this change in marriage began in 1970—about the same year that our church started losing membership and we began losing touch with the next generation.

Studies of the emerging generation seem to agree that the ages of eighteen to thirty, that is, the threshold of adulthood, have become more complex, disjointed, and confusing than in past decades. In his book *Emerging Adulthood* (Oxford University Press, 2004), Jeffrey J. Arnett notes that young adults today put a high premium on finding their identity in an uncertain world. They are impressed with economic and political instability and live their lives accordingly. They focus much more on the self and less upon groups, and they tend to be overwhelmed by their sense of possibilities.

This summer I also read James L. Heft's *Passing on the Faith: Transforming Traditions for the Next Generation of Jews, Christians, and Muslims* (Fordam University Press, 2006). Adults who grew up in the church retain very little of what the church taught them, says Heft. Our churches have not passed on the faith to our children. (The chances that someone who grew up in The United Methodist Church will still be United Methodist by age thirty are something like one in six. For Episcopalians, Presbyterians, and many others, the rate of attrition is even worse.)

Jeffrey Arnett agrees with Heft's gloomy analysis of those who happen to have grown up in the church. Arnett says, "The most interesting and surprising feature of emerging adults' religious beliefs is how little relationship there is between the religious training they received throughout childhood and the religious beliefs they hold at the time they reach emerging adulthood." A recent survey showed that today's young adults attend church less, pray less, are less likely to believe in the authority of the Bible, are more likely to identify themselves as non-religious, and tend to be extremely suspicious of institutions and organized religion.

Not too long ago the church could count on a return to church by young adults when they had their first children. That appears not to be a pattern for today's young adults. Because they are postponing marriage, the church can expect at least a twenty-year gap between young adults leaving the church and returning. In her book *Generation Me: Why Today's Young Americans Are More Confident, Assertive, Entitled, and More Miserable than Ever Before* (Free Press, 2006), Janet Twenge depicts this generation of young adults as extraordinarily self-absorbed and narcissistic. Twenge thinks that we parents made a mistake in fostering in our children an aura of self-esteem without giving them realistic assessments of how challenging the adult world would be.

Today's young adults are documented as having a great love of God, but less commitment to a particular religious tradition. When it comes to religion many of them are "dabblers and deferrers." I believe that this is not only one of the most important challenges facing the church with this age group, but also one of our most difficult challenges as United Methodists.

Fortunately, we Wesleyans believe in conversion. We need to know more about what young adults need to be converted from and to. We also must set higher priorities on reaching today's young adults. Young Christians are not a priority for us until every pastor spends as much time with this generation as with older generations, until each congregation shows in its staff, its budget, and its energies that it is really taking seriously our mandate to reach this generation for Christ. With God's help, we can. (October 13, 2008)

RESISTING THE CLUTCHES OF CONSUMERISM

Our government no longer refers to us as "citizens," but as "consumers." If we can get you to consume cigarettes, cars, mouthwash, and sedatives, then we can get you to consume people. That is why Calvin Klein uses soft kiddie porn to sell blue jeans. Consumption.

Therefore the question: "How could we, who confess Jesus Christ as Lord, rather than, say, Michael Eisner as Lord, how can we as a church resist the corrosive acids of capitalism?"

The immediate problem confronting us is that our church is accommodationist. Even though we know that there is a strong, critical strain in Wesleyanism against the evils of "riches," we quickly learned in this society that there is no way to be a successful, responsible, public church without submitting to the political vision that says there is no greater purpose of human community than accumulation and aggrandizement.

For this reason, the "user friendly" approach to church won't work. There is no way to entice people off the streets with hymns that are based on advertising jingles and end up with the cross-bearing, self-sacrificial, burden-bearing Jesus. Evangelism cannot be based upon our basic selfishness ("come to Jesus and get everything you want fixed") and end up with anything resembling historic Christianity.

One of the reasons why church is difficult is that the modern media culture (a culture which has no other purpose than giving us what we want, since "getting what we want" is the main purpose of life) has been so successful in forming us into such consumers.

In the middle of a sermon I once said, "If you bring a child into this church, say a child of four or five, that child will have a difficult time during the service. Church does not come naturally. The child will have to be trained to sing this music, to bend his life toward these stories, to pay attention to that which he quite naturally avoids. If you take that same child into Toys R Us, no training is necessary. Greed comes to us quite naturally. After all, this is America."

But then I caught myself in mid-sentence, and said, "No, that's not quite fair to Toys R Us. Billions have been spent, and our very best talent expended, in forming that child into the habits of consumption. Barney is not innocent."

For me, one of the most moving moments is when people come forward to receive the Lord's Supper. They shuffle forward and hold out their hands to receive the elements of communion. I look into their outstretched empty hands. I say, "I notice that your hands are empty, as if *you* were empty, needing some gift, grace."

They reply to me, "Oh no, not at all. I have my masters degree, a well-fixed pension."

I persist, "That all may be true, but in this moment you look touchingly dependent, as if your life would be nothing if you did not receive a gift."

The good news of the gospel is that such bad news about us is the great good news about God. God is determined to get back what God owns. And we, timid church though we are, are part of God's plan to win back the world.

One night in a Duke dormitory Bible study I had some bad news to deliver—Luke 18:18-26. Jesus meets an upwardly mobile, smart, young man. The students perk up upon meeting one of their own in the Bible. Having kept all the rules so well, the young man is looking for a real spiritual challenge. Jesus says, "Just one little thing is left. Go, sell all you have, give it to the poor, strip down, follow me."

With that the young man got really depressed. Jesus remarks to his students, "It is hard to save these upwardly mobile types. Easier to shove a fully loaded dromedary though the eye of a needle. Impossible! Of course, with God, anything is possible."

I then asked the students what they thought of Jesus' prejudice against wealth.

"Isn't that great?" one said, "Just laid things out so directly. Lots of times with Jesus, you can't figure out what he wants you to do. Here, it's different. I like his candor. He's so clear, almost anybody can figure it out. This guy hears what Jesus is up to and knows he doesn't want any part of it. That's great."

Then another student. "I like the way Jesus believes in him. He invites him to join up. I'm looking for a challenge just now; maybe that's why I like this. Jesus believes in him. Like me, this guy probably can't imagine that it's possible for him to break free, to let go of all that stuff, not to go to law school, not to please his parents. But Jesus thinks he can do it, even him."

That night I learned that sometimes the difference between bad news and good news is where you happen to be when you get the news. The breakdown and dissolution of American culture, otherwise known as Disneyworld, is a gift, a marvelous time for us to attempt to save people before it's too late, to learn to worship a God whose victories come through righteousness, not riches. We get to call everyone to confess that Jesus Christ is the one word of God to whom we must listen in life and in death. (December 4, 2006)

REACHING YOUNG ADULTS

In 1994, a commission convened by the Center on Addiction and Substance Abuse at Columbia University, with Joseph A.

Califano, Jr., as chair, issued a rather alarmist report, "Rethinking Rites of Passage: Substance Abuse on America's Campuses." The report invented the phrase "binge drinking." It noted that one in three college students drinks primarily to get drunk. In a curious perversion of the Women's Movement, the number of women who reported drinking to get drunk more than tripled between 1977 and 1993, a rate now equal to that of men. The Califano report noted that college students spent 5.5 billion dollars a year on alcohol, more than on all other beverages and their books combined. The average student spent $446 on alcohol per year, far exceeding the per capita expenditure for the college library. Not surprisingly, the beer industry targets young adults as its best hope for increasing sales. These trends have continued unabated. Thus NCAA basketball is brought to us by Anheuser Busch.

For youth off campus, the picture is equally disturbing. The rate of violent crimes by youth in the United States rose by 25 percent over the past decade. The teenage suicide rate has tripled over the past three decades. Suicide is the second leading cause of death for 15- to 19-year-olds. The image of our nation's best and brightest mindlessly consuming large amounts of alcohol is not an attractive one. Yet, it is an image which accurately portrays an important aspect of today's young adults.

I have sometimes called today's twenty-something crowd "The Abandoned Generation." Today's young adults have the dubious distinction of being our nation's most aborted generation. After scores of interviews with them, Susan Litwin called them "The Postponed Generation," those children of the children of the Sixties who were raised by parents so uncertain of their own values that they dared not attempt to pass on values to their young.

Here is the way in which Yale's Allan Bloom put the problem: "The souls of young people are in a condition like that of the first men in the state of nature—spiritually unclad, unconnected, isolated, with no inherited or unconditional connection with anything or anyone. They can be anything they want to be, but they have no particular reason to want to be anything in particular."

We have therefore made "reaching a new generation of Christians" one of our Conference priorities. The good news is that many of these young people are willing to listen, amazingly willing to sit still and to focus if we are bold enough to speak. For what could a preacher ask but that? My student generation of the Sixties was unable to hear words spoken by anyone over the age of thirty. Our parents lied to us about Vietnam; they failed to be straight with us about civil rights.

I have found that today's "Abandoned Generation" brings a new curiosity and openness to the gospel as well as a willingness to hear what their elders have to say, if we will speak directly to them. Therefore leaders of the church need to revise some of our conventional wisdom about the imperviousness of young adult hearts to the gospel.

Thomas G. Long, who led this year's Bishop's Convocation, says it well:

> There is a growing recognition that it is not enough for the community of faith to wait around for the "boomers" to drift back.... Conventional wisdom holds that there are three broad phases in religious commitment: there is childhood, a pliable and receptive age religious instruction can and should be given; there is mature adulthood, when people, given the right incentives, can be persuaded to take on the responsibilities of institutional church life. In between childhood and adulthood there is the vast wasteland of adolescence and young adulthood, a time when most people wander or run away from their religious roots. The most that a community of faith can do in this middle period is to wait patiently, to leave people alone in their season of rebellion, smiling with the knowledge that, by the time these rebels arrive at their thirties, they will probably be back in the pews and may well be heading up the Christian education committee.
> This conventional wisdom is wrong.... [3]

Long feels that the contemporary church must take the religious wanderings of young adults with new seriousness, that the time is ripe for new strategies of evangelization and Christian education of a generation who, having been left to their own devices, religiously speaking, now need to be addressed by the church. Can we see the needs and problems of this generation of young adults as an invitation to proclaim the gospel with boldness, to beckon them toward a new world named the kingdom of God? If we can, we shall discover this generation as a marvelous opportunity for gospel proclamation. (November 12, 2007)

NOTES

1. Stanley Hauerwas and William H. Willimon, *Resident Aliens* (Nashville: Abingdon Press, 1989).

2. Ann Tyler, *Saint Maybe* (New York: Ballantine Books, 1996).

3. Tom Long, "Beavis and Butthead Get Saved," *Theology Today* 51, no. 2 (July 1994): 201.

CHAPTER 9

PROVOKING CHANGE

CHRIST MEANS CHANGE: FURTHER
THOUGHTS ON MINISTRY OF CONVERSION

The Christian life comes neither naturally nor normally. Little within us prepares us for the shock of moral regeneration that is occasioned by the work of Christ among us. What God in Christ wants to do in us is nothing less than a radical new creation—movement from death to life. This means that ministry among the baptized tends to be more radical, disruptive, and antagonistic than we pastors admit. We are awfully accommodated, well situated, at ease in Zion, or at least disgustingly content with present arrangements. We reassure ourselves with the comforting bromides of a lethargic church: everyone in mainline Protestantism is in decline; everyone has become geriatric; even the Baptists are losing members; people can't change; you can't teach old dogs new tricks. Sociological determinism has got us. What's to be done?

Despite our settled arrangements with death, as an African American preacher friend of mine puts it, the gospel means, "God is going to get back what God owns." C. S. Lewis spoke of his life before his conversion as "before God closed in on me." Conversion, being born again, transformed, regenerated, detoxified, is God's means of closing in upon us, of getting God's way with the world, despite what that reclamation may cost God, or us.

Deep in my Wesleyan once-warmed heart is a story of how a priggish little Oxford don got changed at Aldersgate and thereafter. John Wesley's life was well formed, well fixed by a host of positive Christian influences upon him before the evening on Aldersgate Street. Yet, what happened afterwards has led us Wesleyans to see his heart "strangely warmed" as nothing less than dramatic ending and beginning, death and birth, a whole new world.

Such a story, fixed deep in our souls, challenges a church that has become accommodated to things as they are, the cultural status quo. It stands as a rebuke to a church that has settled comfortably into a characterization of the Christian life as pleasantly continuous and basically synonymous with being a good person.

Scripture enlists a rich array of metaphors to speak of the discontinuous, discordant outbreak of new life named as "conversion." *Born from above,* or *born anew* (John 3:7; 1 Peter 1:3, 23), *regeneration* (John 3:5; Titus 3:5), *putting on a new nature* (Eph. 4:24; Col. 3:10), and *new creation* (2 Cor. 5:17). Paul contrasts the old life according to the flesh with *life according to the Spirit* (Rom. 8:1-39). Baptism tries to tell us that the Christian life is at times discordant, dissonant, and disrupting. When one joins Rotary or the League of Women Voters they give you a membership card and a lapel pin. When one joins the body of Christ, we throw you under, half drown you, strip you naked, and wash you all over, pull you forth sticky and fresh like a newborn. One might think people would get the message.

But, as Luther said, the Old Adam is a mighty good swimmer. A conversionist faith is so disconcerting, particularly to those for whom the world as it is has been fairly good. Those on top, those who are reasonably well fed and fairly well featured, tend to cling to the world as it is, rather than risk the possibility of something new. For all these economic, social, and political reasons we pastors tend toward the maintenance of stability rather than the expectation of conversion. (January 31, 2005)

NEW CREATION

Paul was stunned by the reality of the resurrection—the way God not only vindicated Jesus by raising him from the dead, but also thereby recreated the entire *kosmos*. In Easter, an old world had been terminated and a new one was being born, so Paul was forced to rethink everything that he had previously thought, including ethics. Much of what Paul says about Christian behavior was formed as his testimony to the resurrection, an event that he had experienced within the dramatic turnaround in his own life.

Whereas Jesus did Easter at the empty tomb, Easter happened to Paul on the Damascus Road. "So if anyone is in Christ, there is a new creation: everything old has passed away; see, everything has become new! All this is from God, who reconciled us to himself through Christ, and has given us the ministry of reconciliation" (2 Cor. 5:17-18). Verse 17, in the Greek, lacks both subject and verb so it is best rendered by the exclamatory, "If anyone is in Christ—new creation!"

Certainly, old habits die hard. There are still, as Paul acknowledges so eloquently in Romans 8, "the sufferings of this present time." It makes a world of difference whether or not one knows the resurrection. Thus, making doxology to God (Rom. 11:33-36), Paul asks that we present ourselves as "a living sacrifice, holy and acceptable to God" by not being "conformed to this world" but by being "transformed by the renewing of your minds" (Rom. 12:1-2).

All of this is resurrection talk, the sort of tensive situation of those who *both* find their lives still in an old, dying world, *and* are yet now conscious of their citizenship in a new world being born. Our lives are eschatologically stretched between the sneak preview of the new world being born among us in the church and the old world where the principalities and powers are reluctant to give way. In the meantime, which is the only time the church has ever known, we live as those who know something about the fate of the world that the world does not yet know—and that makes us different.

CONVERSION AS JUSTIFICATION AND SANCTIFICATION

There are those who might like to have new life, but at their worst, do not want to give up anything for it. Something is gained in conversion to Christ, yet something is lost as well, and the loss can be painful. Although the church has struggled with how to talk about the transformation that occurs in us through the work of Christ, at our best we have spoken of that new life by holding two terms in tension. We Wesleyans have always asserted that conversion is a twofold process of transformation whereby we are *justified*—made right with God through God's redemptive work among us—and *sanctified*—transformed, enlisted, commandeered, joined to the saints—in a lifelong redemptive journey with Christ.

Vatican II spoke of the worship of the church as "the glorification of God and the sanctification of the faithful." While we are praising God in worship, we are being changed, our lives are being transformed by the object of our affections. Among Protestants, Luther tended to stress the power of justification and Calvin stressed the need for sanctification. It was Wesley's theological vocation to attempt to keep these two movements of conversion in tension with each other, stressing the complementarity of justification and sanctification. American, evangelical Protestantism has been guilty, in the past, of making conversion a momentary, instantaneous phenomenon—come down to the altar, confess your sin, and you are instantaneously "saved." The Protestant reformers, on the other hand, tended to think of conversion as a process rather than a moment.

Our culture lives with a fantasy of instantaneous transformation and change without cost. Wade Clark Roof's massive study of contemporary American spirituality depicts a nation where there are many people on a spiritual quest, cobbling together their faith from a patchwork quilt of a little this and a little that, a nation full of people who want the benefits of adherence to a religious tradition with none of the limits. This "spiritual marketplace," as Roof aptly titled it, is a world where the consumer is king, where bits and pieces are extracted from a religious tradition and few demands are made for costly ethical transformation. Though Roof did not put the matter like this, I would characterize the new spiritual market as a place where many would like to be converted, justified without cost, and few desire to be sanctified.

Sanctificationists stress the power of new life in Christ to make us more than we would have been if we had been left to our own devices. We must take up our cross *daily*. The Christian faith takes time, a lifetime to get right. Therefore Calvin speaks of the new life in Christ as "regeneration," understanding new life as a process, as a long-term, life-long inculcation of a set of practices that do not come naturally. Too much of American evangelical Christianity depicts the Christian life as a momentous, one-time turning, an instantaneous event that occurs in our subjective consciousness. But the Reformers were convinced that sin is so deeply rooted in our thinking and willing that only a lifetime of turnings, of fits and starts, of divine dislodgment and detoxification can produce what God has in mind for us. Daily we turn. Daily we are to take up the cross and follow. Daily we keep being incorporated into the body of Christ that makes us more than we could have been if we had been left to our own devices.

NEOTENY

Don Scavelli, director of the Methodist Foundation in Detroit (Don is one of my "outside agitators"), gave me a great new book on management, *Geeks & Geezers: How Era, Values, and Defining Moments Shape Leaders,* by Warren G. Bennis and Robert J. Thomas (Harvard Business School Press, 2002). The book is a study in how generational differences affect our attitudes toward the world and how our age affects the way we lead people. It's mostly a book about business leadership, but I found it to have implications for us clergy who must lead in the church.

"Geeks" are those leaders thirty-five years old and younger—those who are characterized by a "hang loose" style that "goes with the flow," and expect, even enjoy, constant change. "Geezers" are those leaders over sixty who got their leadership training during their time in World War II. They tend to be big on organization, procedure, and careful, cautious decision making. There are, however, similarities among a few within these two generational groups. The authors found a number of "Geezers" who were amazingly youthful in their outlook toward the world. They were creative, adaptive, and innovative even on into their seventies and eighties.

What made these "Geezers" different? The quality that set them apart from their peers was a new word for me: "Neoteny." Bennis says his friend Phil Slater told him "neoteny" was the word that described the exciting and engaging quality that the "Geezers" whom Bennis had interviewed had radiated.

> Later, I asked [Phil] to elaborate, and he answered with an autobiographical e-mail. "I often feel isolated because so many of the people I know," he wrote, "have 'settled' in some way. The world has jelled for them—closed. It no longer has the sense of possibility that it had for many of us as children. The neoteny I was talking about has to do with the fact that some of us have kept that sense of possibility and wonder alive. I'm not sure what all is involved in that or why it happens, but I see it in a lot of successful people (it's why they're so much more fun to talk to about ideas than academics are), and it's very meaningful to me."... This book is about that remarkable quality.[1]

Neoteny is the ability to think young even when one advances in age.

We discovered that every one of our geezers who continues to play a leadership role has one quality of overriding importance: neoteny. The dictionary defines neoteny, a zoological term, as "the retention of youthful qualities by adults." Neoteny is more than retaining a youthful appearance, although that is often part of it. Neoteny is the retention of all those wonderful qualities that we associate with youth: curiosity, playfulness, eagerness, fearlessness, warmth, energy. Unlike those defeated by time and age, our geezers have remained much like our geeks—open, willing to take risks, hungry for knowledge and experience, courageous, eager to see what the new day brings. Time and loss steal the zest from the unlucky, and leave them looking longingly at the past. Neoteny is a metaphor for the quality—the gift—that keeps the fortunate of whatever age focused on all the marvelous undiscovered things to come.[2]

I'm concerned that the average age of the average United Methodist is my age, fifty-eight. I think our church suffers from too much old thinking, too many outmoded means of doing business, and an inability to think of new ways of responding to new challenges. It is no coincidence that most of our leaders (like bishops!) are members of the "Geezer" generation. The average age of our clergy is over forty-five. I therefore think there is a need to cultivate among ourselves a propensity for neoteny!

We serve a living God, a God who constantly invites us toward new life and rebirth. Neoteny—it's a Christian virtue! (April 11, 2005)

LEADING CHANGE IN THE CHURCH

I am convinced that our church is in need of some fundamental changes. I hope to be helpful in leading some of these needed changes here in North Alabama. We need more leaders in our church, particularly pastors, who are willing to dream dreams and think new thoughts, then courageously lead in change. We need bishops who will see their role as change agent, rather than barely maintaining the status quo. It is the nature of the

Christian life to expect conversion and growth and grace. Therefore, it is inevitable that we should change.

However, change in any system, including the body of Christ, must be made with care. In early December, our "outside agitator" was Bill Yon. Bill has had a distinguished career as a church leader within the Episcopal Church, working with Episcopal bishops and with innumerable congregations to make them more effective in ministry. Bill has certainly embodied the ministry of the change agent.

Yet, when he gave advice to me in public as one of our outside agitators, Bill said, "You seem to me as if you are a person who wants to lead in change. You are a pusher and agitator yourself. I, therefore, would like to give you some advice—you need to make yourself a change budget." A change budget? Yon went on to say that all organisms, including the church, have years of dormancy and years of growth. You can look at the statistics for The United Methodist Church and see that it has been in a period of dormancy for some time. I believe that we are poised for a time of growth. No organization, though, can stand constant growth and change, and times of growth must be matched with times of dormancy and stability. You can see this in Jesus' ministry. Jesus is depicted in the Gospels as being on a journey, on the move. But he was not constantly on the move. He had times of quiet reflection, times of withdrawal for prayer and meditation.

When I did a commentary on the Acts of the Apostles, I noted that the church is presented in Acts as constantly on the move. But that is not always the case. There are numerous instances where Paul, after experiencing dramatic evangelistic success and numerous conversions, "remained there for the next two years." Paul didn't simply move constantly; he also stayed where he had experienced so many conversions and began an extended process of teaching and lecture.

So Yon says to those of us who would work change that we must get ourselves a "change budget." He says that he feels that his own church, the Episcopal Church, has presented its members with too many traumatic changes in too short a period of time. Now the organization is paying for it. Our challenge is not simply to change the system, but, through many changes, to produce a more robust system. There must be times of equilibrium if there are to be times of forward movement. In my intent to lead changes in our Conference, I need to keep this in mind.

The local congregation, our members, gives us a certain amount of human capital to be expended in changes. But we must invest that capital wisely. It is possible to push an organization so far toward innovation that the organization reacts negatively, withdraws, solidifies, and devotes its energies to resisting all change. In order to avoid this, we must, therefore, exercise our changes wisely, exercise care for the needs of an organization to move forward, and then achieve some measure of stability. Jesus not only challenged his disciples to move forward but he also encouraged times of withdrawal and prayer, and we ought to do the same. (May 2, 2005)

BEYOND THE BOUNDARIES

The majority of United Methodist churches in North Alabama are small churches and they are in precipitous decline. All indications are that the decline will accelerate over the next decade, despite our efforts, and despite the mandate of Jesus Christ that we, as his disciples, are to go and to grow. By my estimates, we produce about twenty new small churches every year in North Alabama, as once–medium-sized churches shrink.

History shows that small congregations are wonderfully resilient. They survive. To be honest, one reason United Methodism has more small membership churches than any other denomination is that we have so many ways of subsidizing and supporting small churches, long after any other denomination would have forsaken these small congregations.

However, one of the main reasons that small churches survive is that many so restrict their view of the ministry of the church, scaling down their expectations for discipleship, that clergy and laity find it easy to meet the meager expectation that many people have for the small church. If your definition of the church does not extend beyond the bounds of the nurture and care of the people in that congregation, then it doesn't take much pastoral leadership, or much time and effort, to meet those expectations.

Now if we move from our scaled-down, limited expectations for the church, to Jesus' more expansive expectations, many of our small congregations look quite different. *The major reason why our small congregations are not growing, and the major reason why most small churches are almost exclusively tied to those of us in the over-fifty generation, is that they have limited their ministry to the boundaries of their congregation.* Many of our small churches are "church family," as we like to say. That family feel of the small church becomes the very reason why a small congregation eventually dies.

Veteran church observer Penny Marler has studied small congregations. She notes that it is very difficult, virtually impossible, for a long-established small congregation to grow—*mainly because it restricts its ministry to its own people.* A congregation may think of itself as a loving and caring group of people, but if you visit there on a Sunday morning, or if you should try to join, you have the impression that they are unfriendly, focused inward, and closed. Their vision of the church is restricted to those people whom God gave them thirty years ago. They restricted their ministry to the members of the church, and their families. As those members age, as the birth rate declines, so do these churches.

Alas, too many of us pastors have bought into this view of ministry. We believe that the purpose of our ministry is to care for the people within the congregation exclusively. We pray for the sick, we visit the infirm, we focus upon the needs of the congregation, without praying for, visiting, or encountering anyone beyond the bounds of the congregation. And the congregation comes to value a pastor exclusively on that pastor's performance within the congregation. Death is the result.

The writer to the Hebrews speaks of Jesus Christ as the one who went "outside the camp." Jesus Christ was crucified in great part because he went beyond the boundaries. He reached out, touched, and embraced the untouchables. He was constantly pushing out beyond the boundaries, expanding the notion of God's kingdom and God's people. In fidelity to Jesus Christ, we must stop propping up small congregations who have decided to limit their vision of the church to those who happen to have been given to them by a previous generation. And pastors who have come to limit their definition of ministry to those within the bounds of a congregation have got to grow in their definition of what God has called them to do as evangelical leaders of the church. Any congregation that limits its ministry to itself will not be with us long into the future. This appears to be a law of church growth and decline. More important, it also seems to be an implication of following a Savior like Jesus! (August 20, 2007)

NOTES

1. Warren G. Bennis and Robert J. Thomas, *Geeks & Geezers: How Era, Values, and Defining Moments Shape Leaders* (Harvard Business School Press, 2002), xii.

2. Ibid., 20.

CHAPTER 10

THE PROBLEM OF SIN

SIN

The created order is designed for the well-being of all creatures and as a place of human dwelling in covenant with God. As sinful creatures, however, we have broken that covenant, become estranged from God, wounded ourselves and one another, and wreaked havoc throughout the natural order. We stand in need of redemption.

We United Methodists have only recently gotten a reputation for having a rather rosy view of humanity. The longer Methodist view and the official positions of our church paint a different picture. We've never taken as bleak a perspective on the human condition as our Calvinist precursors, but still, right at the beginning of our theological reflection we admit that things are bad between us and God and among ourselves. When asked to list the absolutely essential beliefs of Methodists, John Wesley was remarkably brief: "(1) original sin, (2) justification by faith alone, (3) holiness of heart and life." Note that Wesley begins with honest confession that we are, despite any of our good intentions, *sinners*.

How did we get the world, the way it is? Our beliefs as Christians don't tell us much about *how* the world got here; we leave that to the scientists. Yet we do believe that we know *why* there is something rather than nothing. "In the beginning when God created the heavens and the earth...God saw everything that he had made, and indeed, it was very good" (Gen. 1:1, 31). Our world is God's idea. All life is here for a good reason, a purpose. We get an early glimpse of that purposeful creation in Genesis (the first book of the Bible, whose name means "Beginning"). "God said, 'Let us make humankind in our image'" (Gen. 1:26). While theologians argue over just to what "in our image" refers—reason, spirit, humor?—United Methodists state that purpose is *"dwelling in covenant with God."* Something there is within the purposes of God that makes God invite us to join in God's work in the world. Thus God gave the first humans, creatures though they were, a command to care for God's good garden that is the world and to "be fruitful and multiply," to propagate and to create in a way that shares some divine creativity with God.

And yet very early, at the dawn of our history with God, things went badly wrong. Not content to be creatures, we attempted various ways of becoming gods unto ourselves, Promethean self-creators rather than creatures of the Creator. Discontent to be coworkers with God, we rebel, disobey, and take the world into our own hands. Soon after the primal couple produced children, one of the children became the first fratricide (Gen. 4) when Cain murdered his brother Abel. Our bloodletting and head-bashing is congenital.

We have broken that covenant, become estranged from God, wounded ourselves and one another, and wreaked havoc throughout the natural order. Read your morning newspaper, take Western History 101, visit your city dump, look within your own heart, and you will see why we need not belabor or argue a major United Methodist belief: *we are sinners.* Here's Wesley on our condition:

> We are already bound hand and foot by the chains of our own sins. These, considered with regard to ourselves, are chains of iron and fetters of brass. They are wounds wherewith the world, the flesh, and the devil have gashed and mangled us all over. They are diseases that drink up our blood and spirits that

bring us down. . . . But considered, as they are here, with regard
to God, they are debts, immense and numberless. Well, therefore, seeing we have nothing to pay, may we cry unto him that
he would "frankly forgive" us all.[1]

We did not turn out as God intended. "Prosperity Theology"
purveyed by popular TV preachers notwithstanding, we really are
not right.

Here, having just crossed the threshold from perhaps the
bloodiest, cruelest century ever into the terrorism and the wars
against terrorism of our nascent century, well, we are not off to a
particularly good future, are we? Still, all evidence to the contrary, some blithely assert that humanity is basically good, that
we are all doing the best we can, that down deep, we mean well
and we are, when all is said and done, making progress. At first
such optimistic assertions seem superficial and silly, and indeed
they are. But then, a chief aspect of our sinfulness is to deny that
we are, after all, down deep, when all is said and done, *sinners*!

And so, in the "fullness of time" (Galatians 4:4) the same God
who made promises to us and who kept forgiving us when we
broke our promises, the same God who kept coming back to
Israel and resuming the conversation that we, by our sin, had
ended, this Holy and Righteous One lovingly moved in with the
profane and the unrighteous. "The Word became flesh and lived
among us" (John 1:14). We could not come to God, so God came
to us. We could not, by our efforts, climb up to God, so God con-
descended to us. For United Methodist Christians, salvation has
a face, a name, a particular way of living and dying and rising and
being present. That name is Jesus. We believe not only that we
are sinners but also that, in Jesus Christ, God Almighty did something decisive about our sin. (July 16, 2007)

SIN IN CHRISTIAN MINISTRY

A number of years ago I gave a series of lectures at a pastors'
school on the West Coast. My subject: sin and its consequences.

My remarks were not universally well received. A number in my audience—mostly men, middle aged, mainline Protestants—seemed rather baffled by my presentations, hurt even. After all, they seemed to say, we are educated, enlightened, socially progressive folk living in the Pacific Northwest who have overcome gloomy matters like sin that once were so overstressed by orthodox Christianity. Onward and upward, better and better every day in every way, that's our motto.

Among those who heard me gladly was a group of clergywomen. At first this surprised me. A number of feminist theologians back then were quite critical of Augustinian preoccupation with sin, particularly the sin of pride, saying that such concern was oppressive to the full self-expression of women. But in talking with these clergywomen about their experiences in the pastoral ministry I realized a cold truth: if one is on top, well-fixed, secure, then one can afford to be sanguine about sin. People in power always think of ourselves as basically good people living in a well-ordered world. Why not? It is *our* world. To such folk, "prophetic ministry" means mostly minor tinkering with the present political structures, the passage of new legislation, helpful advice to Congress. Our world, while needing certain modifications, is basically good because it is *our* world.

But if one is on the bottom, at times victim of other people's cruelty and disregard, then one tends to have a different view of the world. As one of these clergywomen put it, "there is no way to explain how such nice people, the sort of people I have in my congregation, could be so mean—except that they are sinners." These women, having been called to ministry, were finding the church to be a risky place. The traditional Christian sense of sin made new sense to them. As Kierkegaard noted, "sin presupposes itself" into human endeavor, even (especially) endeavor that is ecclesiastical.

In his *People of the Lie*, Scott Peck says that if one is looking for genuine evil, then one ought to look first within the synagogue and church. It is of the nature of evil to "hide among the good." Satan masquerades as an angel of light. Lucifer is his name, after all. Leaders of the church beware, not only because we work among the godly, but also because we ourselves, called to speak to and for God to God's people, are in a morally vulnerable position where sin is always lurking about the door (Gen. 4:7).

A friend of mine, an economist, was asked to serve on the board of a church charitable organization that helps needy children. His first days on the board were a sort of religious conversion experience, so inspired was he by the work of the organization, so impressed was he by the tremendous amount of need. But then he learned of the salaries, the real salaries of some of the clergy staff. He uncovered accounting irregularities. After prayerful consideration, he brought it to the attention of the directors and...he was dismissed from the board.

He told me, "I think clergy, because they tell themselves that they are doing the work of the Lord, are particularly susceptible to self-deceit. If you're feeding hungry children, none of the moral rules apply to you that apply to other mere mortals." If you are visiting the sick, preaching the truth, offering up the Body and Blood of Christ, who is there within the congregation or even among your clergy peers to judge you?

For all these reasons, we clergy must cultivate a robust doctrine of sin—our own and the church's—or clergy are dangerous. Although sin appears to be a neglected aspect of much contemporary theology, the practice of ministry requires a healthy appreciation for the ubiquity of sin in the church and its leaders. As C. S. Lewis noted, "it is the policy of the Devil to persuade us there is no Devil." It is a sure sign of a compromised church—a church that has retired from the battle with the principalities and powers, a church without prophets—when one finds a church that has stopped dealing with sin.

So Luther advised us to "sin boldly," that is, to sin as those who respect the power of sin because we expect the power of God in Jesus Christ to enable even people like us to admit our sin, to confess our faults, and to be forgiven of our sin. (April 25, 2005)

DESPAIR AS SIN

Some time ago a pastor asked me, "Do you really believe that we can change our system for the better? I just don't think that change is possible for an entrenched system like ours."

One of our greatest challenges, in the present moment, is not to despair, not to believe that new life, change, and renewal are impossible. Here are some thoughts about the implications of Easter for our belief in the possibility of new life.

Because of Easter, we are not permitted despair. There is certainly enough failure and disappointment in the church to understand why depression, disillusionment, and despair could be considered the three curses of pastoral ministry. Despair is most understandable among some of our most visionary and dedicated pastors. Any pastor who is not tempted by despair has probably given in to the world too soon, has become too easily pleased by and accommodated to present arrangements. Daily confrontation with the gap between who God has called the church to be and what the church actually is leads many of our best and brightest to despondency. We grieve for the church.

Yet, as Paul says, we do not grieve as those who have no hope. If our hope were in ourselves or our techniques for the betterment of the church, we might as well abandon all hope. Our hope is in Christ, who for reasons known fully only to him, has determined the church as the major form of his visible presence in the world. Many days I do not know why, and many days I see no evidence for such faith in us. Yet by the grace of God, I do so believe. In Jesus Christ, God is reconciling the world to himself. And Easter tells us that God's purposes shall not be defeated: neither by Satan nor by death nor by principalities and powers, not even by the church itself.

There is that sort of pastoral despair that leads some of our brothers and sisters to quit. Yet there is also that despair, which I find more widespread, that leads some of us to slither into permanent cynicism about the church. In my efforts to reform and to renew my own denomination, at first I thought that much of the resistance I encountered was due to the conservative, reactionary ways of leaders of the church. The powerful always tend to protect the status quo, to preserve the power arrangements that put them in their place. We have never done it that way, and all that.

Upon further reflection, I saw some of their resistance to change as due to the cynical belief that we cannot change, that God either will not or cannot do any new thing with us. It is sad to see accommodation to sin and death. How do we know that Easter is not true? Who told us that Jesus used bad judgment when he made us his witnesses even to the ends of the earth?

In J. F. Powers's novel *The Wheat That Springeth Green,* an old, overworked priest is finally sent a curate to help him care for his parish. The curate cannot type, does not keep regular office hours, and is no help in the old priest's attempt to climb out of the mire of his horribly boring, humdrum round of priestly duties. The old priest explains reality to the young curate. Sweeping his hand across the expanse of the cluttered office, he rages, "This— *all* this—isn't my idea of the priesthood. But this is how it is, Bill, and how it's going to be. This is *it*, Bill—the future. I'm sorry."[2] In order for the powers-that-be to have their way with us, to convince us that the rumor of resurrection is a lie, they must first convince us that death is "reality," and that wisdom comes in uncomplaining adjustment to that reality—"This is *it*."

The theologian Jurgen Moltmann once said that if one considers the evidence for the resurrection of Jesus, it is difficult to see why anyone would disbelieve it, except for two reasons: the resurrection is an odd occurrence, outside the range of our usual experience, so that makes it difficult for our conceptual abilities. Perhaps more important, if Jesus is raised from the dead, then we must change. Resurrection carries with it a claim, a demand that we live in the light of this stunning new reality. Now we must either join in God's revolution or else remain unchanged, in the grip of the old world and its rulers, sin and death. (March 21, 2005)

SINNERS

> When the Pharisees saw this, they said to his disciples, "Why
> does your teacher eat with tax collectors and sinners?" But
> when he heard this, he said, "Those who are well have no need
> of a physician, but those who are sick.... For I have come to
> call not the righteous but sinners." (Matthew 9:11-13)

I stand at the front door of the church. It is Sunday. I like to stand
here and watch people entering the church. What unites them?

Sinners come in the church. Some are still in their mother's
arms. Sleeping, they come, but not of their own volition. They
look innocent enough, but they are still sinners. Though out-
wardly cuddly and cute, they are among the most narcissistic and
self-centered in the congregation. When they wake up, they will
cry out, not caring that the rest of us are about important religious business. When they are hungry, they will demand to be
fed, now. Cute, bundled up, placidly sleeping or peevishly
screaming. Sinners.

Sinners come to church. They are being led by the hand. They
do not come willingly. Though they put up a fight an hour ago, a
rule is a rule, and there they are. They have said that they hate
church. They have said things about church that you wouldn't be
allowed to have published in the local newspaper, if you were
older. Ten years old they are, and they lack experience and
expertise, but not in one area: they are sinners.

Sinners come in the church. Sullen, slouched, downcast eyes.
They were out with friends last night to a late hour, and the
incongruity between here in the morning and there last night is
striking. They know it and it is only one of the reasons why they
do not want to be here. Dirty thoughts. Desire. Things you are
not supposed to think about. These thoughts make these sinners
very uncomfortable at church.

Sinners come to church, and they have put on some weight,
middle-aged, receding hairlines, "showing some age." They are
holding on tight. Well-dressed, attempting to look very
respectable, proper. Youthful indiscretions tucked away, put

behind them, does anybody here know? A couple of things tucked away from the gaze of the IRS. And a night that wasn't supposed to happen two conventions ago. These sinners are looking over their shoulders. They are having trouble keeping things together. Maybe that is why there are so many of these sinners here, coming in the door of the church.

Sinners come in the church, and the doors at last are closed. The last of them scurry to their appointed seats. The organ music begins, played by an extremely talented, incredibly gifted artist, who is also a sinner. And the lyrics to that first hymn, something about "Amazing Grace," sung, appropriately, by those who really need it, need it in the worst way. They sing in the singular, but it ought to be in the plural. "Amazing grace that saved wretches like us."

Sinners come into church. And now for the chief of them all, the one most richly dressed, most covered up, the one who leads, and does most of the talking. Some call him pastor. Down deep, his primary designation is none other than that of those whom he serves. Sinners come into the church, and now their pastor welcomes them, their pastor, the one who on a regular basis presumes to speak up for God, making him the "chief of sinners."

Sinners come to church, all decked out, all dressed up, all clean and hopeful. Sinners, sinners hear the good news, "Christ Jesus came into the world to save sinners" (1 Timothy 1:15). Jesus called as his disciples Matthew, Mark, Luke, and John, Mary and Mary Magdalene. Sinners. Only sinners. And Jesus got into the worst sort of trouble for eating and drinking with sinners. Only sinners. Sinners.

Jesus saves sinners. Thank God. Only sinners. We sinners. (April 6, 2009)

NOTES

1. Frank Baker, ed., *The Bicentennial Edition of the Works of John Wesley* (Nashville: Abingdon Press, 1990), 1:586.
2. J. F. Powers, *The Wheat That Springeth Green* (New York: Alfred A. Knopf, 1988), 175.

CHAPTER 11

ADVENTURES IN PASTORAL MINISTRY

BE WHERE YOU ARE, OR LEARNING TO LOVE THE LOCAL

We United Methodists like to brag that we have more churches than the U.S. has post offices. That means that we have many churches in very small places. American Protestantism has been and, to a remarkable degree, continues to be a rural and small-town phenomenon. For many United Methodist pastors the great challenge of the pastoral ministry is the challenge of life spent outside the big city and the sprawling metropolis.

Life amid the rural, the local, and the provincial can be a challenge. I recall the bishop who told me that, when asked, two-thirds of his pastors indicated that they wished to serve churches in either suburban or urban communities. Yet the bishop's diocese was two-thirds rural. "That means the majority of pastors will be unhappy for the majority of their ministry." Life spent on the margins, far from the "madding," or innovating, crowd—not much to look forward to in that. Except, perhaps, for us preachers.

Preachers must not only worry over the biblical text, carefully exegeting and interpreting Scripture, we must also know people and examine life. Being placed out on the margins, in some country crossroads, may be positively providential for preachers.

My friend Doris Betts, writer of some fine, even *Christian* fiction, can't imagine writing from any better vantage point than her farm in Pittsboro. One day, commuting to teach at the University of North Carolina, she came upon an overturned chicken truck. Chickens, who had never known freedom, were hopping free, perching along the roadside. Some had met their end in the crash. Others were being scooped up, purloined by passersby who had stopped, not to help the frantic farmer chase chickens but to help themselves to a free hen. Doris says it was quite a sight. She went home and began work on her *Souls Raised from the Dead.*

I recall Eudora Welty, as Methodist as Doris is Presbyterian, who was asked, "Why don't you move to New York where you can be in the middle of the literary scene?" She responded by picking up and reading aloud a Jackson, Mississippi, newspaper headline that read, "Man Kills Wife after Sunday School." "Now where am I to get material like that in New York?" she asked.

Ponder the predominance of good writers in small towns and ask, Why? It is perhaps because a writer must know human nature at close range, not in general but in particular, one life at a time, not in the abstract but in the concrete. In the big city, one's observation is limited to those few people with whom one comes into contact at work. In the rural community, everybody knows everybody, and everybody knows everything about everybody.

I encountered much more diversity (that is, really strange, exotic people) in a town of eight thousand than in a city of two hundred thousand. In the village, you can't get away from anybody. You must live with, get your car fixed by, and have your teeth cleaned by these people, even if many of them are not to your liking. In such necessity is grace.

Don't expect good novels out of Chicago or San Francisco. Life is too distracting, numbing, and people too evasive. Opportunities for subterfuge are too great! Years ago I recall a novelist telling us, "Nothing bad ever happens to a writer." By this she meant that anything, even life in a one-stoplight town, provides grist for a writer's imagination. A weird person becomes somebody for most people to avoid. For a writer, the same person is called "material for my next novel."

Go ahead. Live in and maybe even love where Providence has placed you. Be thankful and count your blessings. Nothing bad, even Clinton, South Carolina, has ever happened to the observant preacher.

Besides, the way I read the gospel, it appears that God has this thing for small towns. When something divinely good happens, it tends to happen first in Nazareth.

Wishing you a blessed Thanksgiving—wherever you are. (November 21, 2005)

CONTINUING THE JOURNEY

The other day I called my accountant with a tax question. I asked him why he had been out of town. He told me that he was just back from Las Vegas. Las Vegas? "What would a good Methodist person like you be doing in such a place?" I asked. "School," was his reply. "As a C.P.A. I'm required to have forty hours of classroom instruction every single year." Wow. I had not known that accountants required so much continuing education. Then he asked me an embarrassing question: "How many hours of instruction are United Methodist preachers required to have?"

Sometimes laypeople and their questions can be a real pain.

True, the *Discipline* says that we preachers are to have at least fifteen hours of certified continuing education each year, but my impression is that, at least in our Conference, that requirement has been haphazardly upheld. I was talking with a layperson in North Alabama the other day. He was telling me that his Staff-Parish Relations Committee had met with their pastor in order to give him feedback from the congregation. "We told him that we had heard lots of critical comments about his preaching. Some people in the congregation have complained that his preaching is hard to follow, that it is not always inspiring." "And how did your pastor respond?" I asked. "He got defensive and said, 'Look, I've never fancied myself as a preacher. I'm mostly a caring pastor, not a pulpit performer.'

"We told him that no one was asking for a 'pulpit performer,' but we did need a good biblical preacher," said the lay leader. "He just simply said, 'This is the way I preach. People will just have to get used to it.' You clergy seem to feel that you get all you need to be our pastors in seminary. In the real world, people are going back to school and learning new skills. In business your boss comes in and says something like, 'We're going to promote you to be in charge of marketing. But you don't know much about marketing so we are going to send you to a school—we are going to put you with some guys who are experts in marketing.' You clergy need to learn how to keep learning."

I think he had it right. Seminary ought to be the beginning, not the end, of our preparation for ministry. Particularly in the United Methodist system, where clergy move around and are therefore constantly met with new challenges and changing situations, the ability to retool, to grow and to develop, is an important pastoral virtue.

The United Methodist Church has declared that our congregations shall be served by a learned and well prepared clergy. We are not permitted to have clergy serving our churches who are uneducated and untrained in meeting the needs of God's people and in preaching the fullness of the gospel.

I therefore want us to stress clergy continuing education and lifetime learning. I want our congregations to encourage and make possible periodic times for growth and professional development for their pastors. Our Bishop's Convocation on Ministry must be a time of more intense theological engagement. We should not appoint a pastor to a situation in which we do not also provide the means for that pastor to obtain the skills needed to minister in that situation with competence and care.

Jesus calls all of us to follow him on a journey. Constant growth and change are part of being a faithful disciple. Let us encourage one another to grow in grace, in wisdom, and true godliness, even as our Lord has commanded us. (February 21, 2005)

MINISTRY TO THOSE NOT IN CRISIS

I remember hearing the great George Buttrick speak, shortly before he died, saying to us gathered pastors, "Most any pastor can be helpful to people in time of need. It doesn't take a skillful pastor to visit someone in the hospital and be helpful. When people are sick, they are desperate, grateful for any word, even an inadequate word. Even an inept pastor will be well received in a family where the breadwinner has just been laid off from his job, where the mother has just learned that she has cancer, where the troubled teenager has just run afoul of the law."

Buttrick continued, "Such moments, when people are down and desperate, are not really the greatest tests of our ministry. The greatest tests are those moments when people are not down, not desperate, not at the end of their rope. There is where they often find out just how faithful our gospel really is. In those moments, the pastor has the opportunity to become a prophet, to speak a word, not merely of comfort, but of truth.

"So it takes a real pastor," Buttrick continued, "to go into a family where someone has just been promoted to presidency of the local bank and say, 'Mary, I've just gotten the news of your promotion. So I rushed right over knowing that this promotion is placing you in an extremely vulnerable position, as far as your soul is concerned. I wanted to come over and stand beside you during this time of potential temptation. Could we pray?'"

I remember discussing a fellow pastor with a friend. "Joe is really a wonderful pastor," I said. "Every time I go to the hospital, Joe is there. I am utterly amazed by how much he can be available to his people and their needs." My friend replied, "Joe does most of that for Joe."

I thought this a rather severe judgment. My friend continued, "By constantly enmeshing himself in other people's needs, by lurching constantly from crisis to crisis, Joe is preserved from ever having to reflect upon the value of what he is doing. There is a style of ministry, which I fear Joe embodies, of ambulance-chasing, of becoming so engulfed in the crises of others that he never has to ask tough questions of himself and the ultimate value of his ministry."

Most any of us can be helpful to people when they find out that their cherished daughter has not been admitted to the college of her choice. But it takes great pastoral fortitude to be present with a family when their son has just received his acceptance to Harvard. It takes a real prophet to help people see how we are, spiritually speaking, most vulnerable and at risk in moments of success, power, and accomplishment.

Most of us, as pastors, spend much of our time with people who are relatively content, relatively happy, and more or less at ease. These people, and their contentment, may be our greatest pastoral challenge. Thank you, North Alabama. (October 5, 2005)

THE POINT OF PASTORAL MINISTRY: LAY MINISTRY

Bill Easum, our consultant in ministry in North Alabama, has a provocative word about the need to empower the laity to do ministry:

> "You know, one of the issues here is that everyone relies too much on the pastor to do all the ministry." Before I could finish the man blurted out, "I'm aware our pastor needs help, but we can't afford to hire any more staff." I couldn't let that one go unanswered, so I responded, "I've never met a pastor who needed help. You don't need more staff. All you need to do is equip your congregation to do ministry." For a brief moment the man looked at me dumbfounded and perplexed. Then with a hint of sadness in his voice he uttered the most despicable statement a Christian can make: "But we're just laypeople. We're not called to the ministry and we certainly aren't professionals."[1]

One of the regrettable results of our United Methodist stress on careful preparation and collegial accrediting for our pastors is that there has been a steady "professionalizing" of ministry.

Easum makes the flat, direct statement, "I've never met a pastor who needed help. You don't need more staff."[2] We pastors ought to see ourselves not as the "ministers," but rather as coaches and equippers of those who are called to the ministry of Christ—the laity, the people of God. Years ago, a friend of mine said that if laypersons spend more than fifteen hours out of their week at church, their time's been wasted. Their ministry isn't to be the pastor's "gofer"; it's to follow Christ in ministry in the world. The opposite, he said, was true of pastors. We've wasted our time just as much if we spend more than fifteen hours per week working in the world. That's the laity's calling, and it's too difficult to do without being properly equipped. And that, in turn, is *our* job as pastors: to equip layfolk for the work in the world to which God called them at baptism.

So that implies that the test for our pastoral ministry is not, "How much have I been able to accomplish at my church?" but rather, "How much have I enabled the laity to accomplish at their church?" (March 26, 2007)

NOTES

1. Bill Easum, with Linnea Nilsen Capshaw, *Put On Your Own Oxygen Mask First: Rediscovering Ministry* (Nashville: Abingdon Press, 2004), 14.
2. Ibid.

CHAPTER 12

ORDINATION AND NEW CLERGY

ADVICE FOR NEW PASTORS

Allan Hugh Cole, professor at Austin Presbyterian Seminary, has edited a book for new pastors, From Midterms to Ministry (Eerdmans). I was asked to write a chapter in the volume, recounting my own journey from seminary to the parish, drawing out any implications that my experience had for new pastors. This month, thousands of new pastors will emerge from seminary, a few of them coming to join the ranks of the North Alabama Conference. I therefore offer these thoughts in the next few weeks, hoping that they will be helpful to those of us who are new in the pastoral ministry and those who are not.

Recently, I asked a group of our best and brightest new pastors what they would like most from the church and from me as their bishop. I was surprised to hear them all respond: "Supervision!" They yearn for help with the move between these two worlds because they realize the inadequacy of their preparation. Churches and judicatories must take this move more seriously and must develop better means of mentoring and supervising new pastors through this process.

As someone who now works with new pastors on that move from the world of the theological school to the world of the parish, I have some specific suggestions. First, devise ways to learn to speak their language. Laity sometimes complain that their young pastor, in sermons, uses "religious" words like "spiritual practice," "liberation," "empowerment," "intentional community" (this is an actual list a layperson collected and sent to me) that no one understands and no one recalls having heard in Scripture. Such "preacher talk" makes the pastor seem detached, alien, and aloof from the people and hinders leadership.

At the same time, prepare yourself to become a teacher of the church's peculiar speech to a people who may have forgotten how to use it. This may seem contrary to my first suggestion. My friend Stanley Hauerwas says that the best preparation for being a pastor today is previously to have taught high school French. The skills required to drill French verbs into the heads of adolescents are the skills that pastors need to teach our people how to speak the gospel. Trouble is, most seminarians are more skilled, upon graduation from school, to be able to describe the world anthropologically than theologically. They have learned to use the language of Marxist analysis or feminist criticism better than the language of Zion. We must be persons who lovingly cultivate and actively use the church's peculiar speech.

Keep telling yourself that the difference in thought between the laity in your first parish and that of your friends back in seminary is not so much the difference between ignorance and intelligence; it's just different ways of thinking that arise out of life in different worlds. I recommend reading novels (Flannery O'Connor saved me in my first parish by writing true stories that sounded like they were written by one of my parishioners) in order to appreciate the thought and the speech of people who, while having never been initiated into the narrow confines of the world of theological education, are thinking deeply.

Remind yourself that while the seminary has an important role to play in the life of the church, it is the seminary that must be accountable to the church, not vice versa. It is my prejudice that if you have difficulty making the transition from seminary to parish it is probably a criticism of the seminary. The Christian faith is to be studied and critically examined only for the purpose of its embodiment. Christians are those who are to become that which we profess. The purpose of theological discernment is not to devise something that is interesting to say to the modern world but rather to rock the modern world with the church's demonstration that Jesus Christ is Lord and all other little lordlets are not. (May 11, 2009)

ADVICE FOR NEW PASTORS 2

Here is the rest of my list of unsolicited advice for those moving from seminary to parish. First, be open to the possibility that the matters that were focused upon in the course of the seminary curriculum, the questions raised and the arguments engaged, might be a distraction from the true, historic mission and purpose of the church and its ministry.

On the other hand, be open to the possibility that the church has a tendency to bed down with mediocrity, to accept the mere status quo as the norm, and to let itself off the theological hook too easily. One reason why the church needs theology explored and taught in its seminaries is that theology (at its best) keeps making Christian discipleship as hard as it ought to be. Theology keeps guard over the church's peculiar speech and the church's distinctive mission. Something there is within any accommodated, compromised church (and aren't they all, in one way or another?) that needs to reassure itself, "All that academic, intellectual, theological stuff is bunk and is irrelevant to the way the church really is."

The way the church "really is" is faithless, mistaken, cowardly, and compromised. It's sad that it is up to seminaries to offer some of the most trenchant and interesting critiques of the church. Criticism of the church ought to be part of the ongoing mission of a faithful church that takes Jesus more seriously and itself a little less so. I pray that your theological education rendered you permanently uneasy with the church. Promise me that throughout your ministry you will never be happy with the church.

I pray that you studied hard in seminary, read widely, thought deeply, because you are going to need all of that if you are going to stay long as a leader of the church. Your life would be infinitely easier and less complicated if God had called you to be an accountant or a seminary professor. Most of the stuff that you read in seminary will only prepare you really to grow and to develop after you leave seminary. Think of your tough transition into the parish as the beginning, not the end, of your adventure into real growth as a minister. Theology tends to be wasted on the young. It's only when you run into a complete dead end in the parish, when you are aging and tired and fed up with the people of God (and maybe even God too), that you need to know where to go to have a good conversation with some saint in order to make it through the night.

Believe it or not, it's much easier to begin in the ministry, even considering the tough transition between seminary and the parish, than it is to continue in ministry. A winning smile, a pleasing personality, a winsome way with people, none of these are enough to keep you working with Jesus, preaching the word, nurturing the flock, looking for the lost. Only God can do that and a major way God does that is through the prayerful, intense reading, study, and reflection that you can only begin in three or four years of seminary.

Try not to listen to your parishioners when they attempt to use you to weasel out of the claims of Christ. Much of the criticism that you will receive, many of their negative comments about your work, are just their attempt to excuse themselves from discipleship. "When you are older, you will understand," they told me as a young pastor. "You have still got all that theological stuff in you from seminary. Eventually, you'll learn," said older, cynical pastors. Now it's, "Because you are a bishop, you don't really understand that I can't. . . ." God has called you to preach and to live the gospel before them and they will use any means to avoid it. Be suspicious when people encourage you to see the transition from seminary to the parish as mainly a time finally to settle in and make peace with the "real world." Jesus Christ is our definition of what's real and there is much that passes for "the way things are" in the average church that makes Jesus want to grab a whip in hand and clean house.

The next few years could be among the most important in your ministry, including the years that you spent in seminary, because they are the years in which you will form your habits that will make your ministry. That's one reason why I think the Lutherans are wise to require an internship year in a parish, before seminary graduation, for their pastors and why I think that a great way to begin your ministry is as someone's associate in a team ministry in a larger church. In a small, rural church, alone, with total responsibility on your shoulders, in the weekly treadmill of sermons and pastoral care, if you are not careful there will be too little time to read and reflect, too little time to prepare your first sermons, so you develop bad habits of flying by the seat of your pants, taking shortcuts, and borrowing from others what ought to be developed in the workshop of your own soul. Ministry has a way of coming at you, of jerking you around from here to there, so you need to take charge of your time, prioritize your work, and be sure that you don't neglect the absolute essentials while you are doing the merely important. If you don't define your ministry on the basis of your theological commitments, the parish has a way of defining your ministry on the basis of its selfish preoccupations, and that is why so many clergy are so harried and tired today. Mind your habits. (May 18, 2009)

GATEKEEPERS INTO THE PASTORAL MINISTRY

In our United Methodist system the Board of Ordained Ministry serves as our "gatekeepers" in the admission of persons as pastors in our Connection. I've met with our North Alabama Board of the Ordained Ministry. They have an awesome task in deciding just whom to put forward for ordination and whom to guide toward some other ministry in the church. I've recently read a book that has some interesting insights for these "gatekeepers" and their deliberations about candidates for the ministry.

I share these insights with you because our church is always dependent upon the wise and inspired selection of a new generation of pastoral leadership.

Each person who comes before the gatekeepers is ultimately a mystery of human nature, a thou. When the gatekeepers face such a person they experience essentially insurmountable gaps in their prognostication. Biographical particulars are lost or forgotten, subconscious forces wait to surface, and biological factors remain undetected or are not understood. There are eccentricities of cultural contexts, changes in the meaning of "meaningful," and movement in the overriding structures of history. The sum of these gaps is not an unfortunate disease needing a cure. It is a fact of existence that begs for a positive theological interpretation, the kind of interpretation that assumes that God constantly raises up new leaders among us who bring us new possibilities.

An encounter with one called by God is always also an encounter with God. Gatekeepers must lean close and listen intently for a voice behind the human voices of the women and men who come before them claiming a call to church leadership.

If God really called this person to lead the people of God at this moment in their history, and if God has appointed this person to appear before the gatekeepers, then what message does God also have for the gatekeepers? Is it a message of judgment? Perhaps it is time for them to surrender some of the tedious gatekeeper games of wrangling over agendas that have more to do with the vagaries of pop psychology or half-remembered theology than with the rich depths and subtle contours of the biblical call language. Perhaps it is time to receive candidates for ministry with an empirical inquisitiveness born in the acquaintance with the dialectic drama of the biblical call narratives. In the same way that every church would call itself a friendly church, every group of gatekeepers probably regards itself as biblically grounded for the work it does. What little research there is on the matter tells a different story.

Is God speaking a message of grace to the gatekeepers? In sending certain persons to them, is God allowing gatekeepers a glimpse of some new direction God intends for the institutional church? That Generation X person who speaks from a radically different experience of life in a mainline church may challenge that Baby Boomer–generation gatekeeper to listen with new ears. Sometimes the person who best registers the church's pressing adaptive challenge is located on the periphery and is being nudged to the center of action by God. These peripheral candidates for ministry are of an ethnic group, economic class, or culture niche not yet reached by the church. They will require some sheltering and encouragement along the way. They challenge gatekeepers less at the point of conscience than at the point of imagination. What might God intend in calling such persons? Will the gatekeepers cooperate with God's preferred future for the church?

The seemingly endless parade of new persons appearing before the gatekeepers claiming a call to church leadership from God is a phenomenon of divine stewardship worth pondering. In the face of dire predictions for the church, apparently God continues to call persons to invest their lives in this institution. To use an old-fashioned image that combines mission and risk, God remains in the work of enlisting recruits for church leadership. How dare gatekeepers or anyone else give up on the church now?

Because God is God, the first work of gatekeepers is to stay alert. They can never tell when the leader whom God summons for the demands of the hour will appear on their doorsteps looking like a shepherd, an eighth son, from the village of Bethlehem, from a family that has no obvious pedigree (1 Sam. 16). (March 7, 2005)

GATEKEEPERS INTO THE PASTORAL MINISTRY 2

In my last email to you I reflected upon the significant role of the "gatekeepers" on our Conference Board of the Ordained Ministry. This is the group that is assigned the important task of deciding who will be received into our Connection as pastors.

We believe that persons must be called into the role of pastor. This is more than a personal career choice, even more than a board deciding. There must be a divinely initiated summons. So an important task of our Board of Ordained Ministry is to work with candidates to discern the validity and the force of divine vocation.

God calls with indifference to human circumstance, convenience, or timing. Human protest is a normal response, but so is the divine persistence in the face of such protest. The first and last work of every leader called by God is to come to terms with the One who calls and with the demands of that call.

That brings to the fore a pressing issue of leadership integrity facing the contemporary church. Routinely persons come before the gatekeepers employing the Bible's dramatic call language to name a perceived disruption in their lives. They say they have been plucked out of a life of obscurity against all odds. They claim that a holy dissatisfaction with their present life has been ignited within them. They say there have been signs and wonders along the way to confirm.

But when these persons turn to the future implications of the call they begin to hesitate and stipulate. "Just three more years until my federal pension kicks in; then I'll be ready." "My husband says we can go anywhere we're sent as long as he can drive home from his business each evening." "Isn't there a church somewhere without a parsonage that would appreciate a pastor who wants to live in his own home?" "A lawyer with a lawyer's bills can't afford too much of a cut in salary." "In five years our children will be grown, and we'll be more flexible."

The church through its gatekeepers has grown accustomed to this language of equivocation. Thirty years ago Alvin Toffler and others forecast a working world of "serial careers." That world has arrived: persons are no longer fated by the vocational decisions or indecision of their twenties, thirties, forties, or even fifties. So why not answer the call to ministry farther down the road? Wasn't Abraham seventy-five when he and Sarah were called from their country and kindred? When second, third, or fourth career persons appear before the gatekeepers it is understandable that they carry more baggage than a twenty-one-year-old fresh from a liberal arts college. What else can gatekeepers do but applaud the apparent, if more complicated, work of God among them?

But gatekeepers are also stewards of the biblical language of the call. They are spokespersons for and defenders of the unequivo-cal character of the God revealed in stories like those in the books of Samuel. God's call in Scripture is unconditional and unyielding. For every person trying to coax a more user-friendly reading of the texts there are others who accept the stringent demands of these texts at face value. There are calls from God to the young and very young which do connect. These calls pre-clude the politics of compromise and remind the church of its better self.

There are other calls from God to more mature persons, which raise havoc with accrued loves, previous commitments, accus-tomed lifestyles, and rational life plans. A physician is called away from his practice, a lawyer from her promising career. A mother is called to nurture the body of Christ as well as her three small children. An owner of a five-generation family business must sell it to give undivided attention to the divine call to church leadership. Casualties of such high altitude turbulence arrive at the meeting table of the gatekeepers and the doors of the seminary all the time. They follow God's call unconditionally, and their stories are impressive.

It is ultimately God who calls persons to this struggle, not the "heavy-handedness" of some polity or the "unrealistic expecta-tions" of some ordaining board. It is ultimately God who has placed us in an irreversible world process where there are irre-trievable losses. A call to ministry that is "missed" at twenty is not happily "fixed" at fifty-five. There is much good in that later call, but also much loss for the delay. It is ultimately God who draws the distinction between those who must be set aside now for full-time leadership in the church and those who will not but may get around to it some day. Gatekeepers do well to keep themselves from becoming triangulated in such disagreements.

The argument between an unyielding God and a reluctant recruit is holy ground. (March 14, 2005)

GOD SEND US PREACHERS

This week the theme of our Annual Conference is empowering a new generation. A highlight of Annual Conference is Ordination, when we will ordain a new group of United Methodist pastors. I've written this hymn for the Commissioning Service this year. Please pray this as a prayer that God will continue to send us a new generation of pastoral leaders to lead our church into the future.

God send us preachers brash and true;
Make them to serve your holy word.
Your summons shall by them be heard.
In sermons bold, we have heard you.
You said the word and there was light,
Made new creation by your voice.
When in your presence we rejoice,
You've come to cheer our darkest night.
Your living word made prophets bold,
The Spirit-giv'n Good News to preach.
None could outrun your Spirit's reach;
Brave preachers spoke as they were told.
God speaks to us by God's own Son.
Salvation preached for all to see.
When truth is told, God's victory,
God's Word made flesh, God's will is done.
Each time a preacher stands to speak,
Whenever hungry hearts are fed,
Your church discovers one more time
That Christians live not just by bread.
Give preachers courage to obey,
In some dead place or silent hell,
The angels' Easter charge, "Go! Tell!"
To call more foll'wers to the Way.

These preachers shield from love of praise;
Ignite their sermons with your fire.
May they not fear their people's ire,
But serve your Word throughout their days.
When hands upon their heads are laid
On this, their commissioning day
May they know now your pow'r to say
That same strong word your saints obeyed.
Lord speak to us, our fears relieve;
Just say the word and we are healed.
Hearing your word is faith revealed,
Though we've not seen, yet we believe! (June 1, 2009)

CHAPTER 13

MINISTERIAL CHARACTER

WEAK CLERGY, WATERED-DOWN CHRISTIANITY

I've said it before, I say it again. Few writers are as tough on us clergy as Søren Kierkegaard, that melancholy Dane. However, few writers better remind me of the high calling to which we clergy have been summoned.

Kierkegaard, here in his *Journals*, notes that in his day clergy had moved from being powerful people in their societies to "being controlled" by the surrounding culture. The result was a desperate attempt on the part of the clergy to be useful, to get a hearing, to appear to be relevant to whatever it was that the culture wanted. Thus was Christianity "watered down," according to Kierkegaard.

The good news is that the situation now calls for clergy who are as tough on ourselves as the gospel is tough on humanity. Lacking the former crutches and accolades of the culture, we now must get our courage strictly from the gospel itself. We clergy must begin by applying the gospel to ourselves before we apply it to others. "Even then," says Kierkegaard, "things may go badly":

As long as the clergy were exalted, sacrosanct in the eyes of men, Christianity continued to be preached in all its severity. For even if the clergy did not take it too strictly, people dared not argue with the clergy, and they could quite well lay on the burden and dare to be severe.

But gradually, as the nimbus faded away, the clergy got into the position of themselves being controlled. So there was nothing to do but to water down Christianity. And so they continued to water it down till in the end they achieved perfect conformity with an ordinary worldly run of ideas—which were proclaimed as Christianity. That is more or less Protestantism as it is now.

The good thing is that it is no longer possible to be severe to others if one is not so towards oneself. Only someone who is really strict with himself can dare nowadays to proclaim Christianity in its severity, and even then things may go badly for him.[1]

Still, all things being considered, being a pastor is a high vocation, a great way to expend a life. The way of Christ is narrow and demanding, but it is also a great gift, even "in its severity."

These are my thoughts, thinking with Kierkegaard looking over my shoulder, as I begin this week of ministry. (November 3, 2008)

SOWING AND HARVESTING IN MINISTRY: THE CASE OF MOSES

On Sundays, after preaching in Duke Chapel and retreating to my appointed perch, the seat behind the second sopranos where the preacher blends into the woodwork, I would often look up during the offering at the stained glass window high above and across from where I sat. As preacher, I sat across from the Moses Window. Hardly anyone else in the Chapel could see it, except for me and the second sopranos.

The window contains scenes from his life—Moses raised by royalty, Moses the angry defender of the oppressed, Moses the liberator, the lawgiver, Moses the leader of Israel to the promised land. But somehow—at about 11:45 on Sunday morning, when I'd finished preaching and as I sat there behind the second sopranos—the sun seemed to highlight one Moses scene more than the rest. It's the last scene in his ministry—Moses held back from entering the promised land. Yahweh let Moses get to the door, but would not allow him to go over the threshold with Israel. Whether or not the stained glass artist of our windows intended to force the preacher to ponder that scene, week-in-week-out, I know not. But it works; when I look at the end of Moses' ministry, I am reminded of my own.

There is a lot of unfulfillment in the church. A great deal of life is spent on the verge, at the door but not over the threshold. Preaching is such a fragile art. Who knows what good it does? For me and for the sopranos, as for Moses, the end of the story is not easily known. They sing, I preach, and God only knows where it all leads, what land of promise will be opened through our ministry. God only knows.

A few years ago, when I did a book on clergy burnout (*Clergy and Laity Burnout*, Abingdon Press, 1989), after interviews with dozens of clergy and those who counsel clergy, I noted that one of the most debilitating aspects of Christian ministry is that there are so few results. If we are not careful, we will begin noting the church parking lot that got paved last year, the 3 percent increase in giving, and call that results. In our better moments we know that we are called to a greater harvest, but the harvest is too slow in coming, if it comes at all. What then for us pastors?

A man I know who works with teachers says that the teachers who are best able to keep at it are those "who are good sowers rather than good reapers." Teachers must be people who find meaning enough in the act of planting the seed and do not insist on the privilege of staying around until harvest. So Paul could boast that others harvested where he had planted. Most of the good we do is good that we will never personally see. How many of those who deeply touched your life with just the right word, the absolutely decisive action, the hand on the shoulder at the essential moment, how many of them did you personally thank? Most of the really important things that are done to us by other people go unacknowledged.

If we are going to keep at Christian ministry, as preachers, as sopranos, or in whatever service God calls us to, we will do so only by having confidence both that God really does convey treasure through us earthen vessels and that God really does put us to good purposes, even though we may not see them clearly, even though we may not enter the promised land of concrete results and visible fulfillment with those whom we have tried to uphold in exodus from here to there. (October 10, 2005)

PASTORAL HUMOR AS A RESOURCE FOR CONSTANCY IN MINISTRY

As I've roamed about the North Alabama Conference these past weeks, listening to you, trying to understand my role as a leader of the Conference, more than one person has said to me, "We like your humor." I'm glad. Not everyone appreciates my humor.

I don't know how anyone could survive in this work without a sense of humor. Over the years I've worried about more than one seminarian who just seemed to be much too serious for his or her own good. As Christians, we are people of the resurrection, therefore we are people who love to laugh, who believe that laughter is a wonderfully life-giving, defiant act full of the grace of God.

Easter is that which enables us to keep going, even in our moral failures, even when being a servant of the Word is difficult. Those who have kept at the Christian ministry longer than I will confirm the essential virtue of humor. One can be a pastor with only modest intellectual abilities, but one cannot remain a pastor for long without a sense of humor. The ability to laugh at life's incongruities, to take God seriously but not ourselves, to embrace the strangeness of our people instead of strangling them to death with our bare hands; this is great grace. Without humor, a bishop could be an insufferable bore, a District Superintendent could be dangerous, and a pastor would be in a perpetual state of depression due to the state of the church.

Humor is the grace to put our problems in perspective, to sit lightly upon our clerical status, to be reminded that Jesus really did need to save us, seeing as we have so little means to save ourselves. Humor is just a glimpse, on a human scale, of the way God looks upon us from God's unfathomable grace. Because of the resurrection, the gospel is enabled to be comedy and not tragedy.

There is a close connection between the disruptive quality of humor and Jesus' primary means of communication, the parable. John Dominic Crossan demonstrated how Jesus' parables assault rather than establish a world. A parable typically takes the predominant, officially sanctioned view of reality within a given culture, the world, and then subverts that world. The surprise endings of many parables are close cousins to the endings of jokes. The gospel, in order to make its way in the world, must subvert the received world.

Because pastors, if they are half faithful, must be forever challenging the received world, effective pastors are often masters at irony, satire, and other forms of linguistic subversion. In fact, sometimes pastors are parables themselves, subversive indicators of a style of life unavailable through more prosaic professions. Sometimes our example to the flock is more disruptive than we know.

There is a clergy couple who asked a congregation to hire both of them for one salary. They promised to work with the congregation to apportion the pastoral duties between them. Their rationale for this creative solution was that both of them wanted to share equally in the raising of their two children. While they did so out of commitment to their own values, they were surprised that what they did was a witness to the congregation that there is a more diverse set of possibilities available to us in marriage and family than in the conventional culture. Their example freed up a number of couples within the congregation to consider other means of ordering their marriages.

Thus, pastoral counselor Charles Gerkin speaks of the pastor as a "parabolic person." By our lives as pastors at our best we make the familiar strange and hint at the possibility of another world beyond the taken-for-granted received world.

Humor is a gift, yet it is a gift that, even if modestly bestowed, can be cultivated. The cultivation of humor is a matter of constant attentiveness to the incongruities between God's will and our own, God's intent for Creation and the world's will for itself. Scripture is a great help. I recommend frequent forays into the Gospel of John. There, the people around Jesus, the beneficiaries of his instruction, hardly ever get the point. Corpses are raised from the dead, water turns to wine just by his presence, and nobody gets a handle on Jesus. The one who eluded the grasp of sin and death will not be constrained by us. And yet, he will, out of love, come to us and eat with us.

Clergy ethics, as Easter ethics, is not primarily a matter of rational weighing of all possible courses of action, considering each alternative, narrowing down our prospects to the one right thing to do. Ethics is also an exercise of the imagination, a disciplined attempt to believe that God really is active in our lives, making a way when we thought there was no way. Through forgiveness, God enables us to act more courageously than if we had been forced always to do right. Our hope for righteousness is based upon our knowledge that on Easter he came back to his disciples, the very ones who had so disappointed and forsaken him, and called them, of all people, to be salt, light, and subversion to the world. What a laugh, a wonderful life-giving laugh! Thus we are free to sin boldly, to dare to represent Christ, to be so presumptuous as to try to hope for sainthood, not because of what we might do but because of what God in Christ has done and will do for us, through us, despite us.

The early fathers spoke of Easter as the great joke that God played on the devil. And the joke is often on us. Thus, when on Sunday, little Easter, we gather to make Eucharist, the church is bold to pray, "Give grace, O heavenly Father, to all bishops and other ministers, that they may, both by their life and doctrine, set forth thy true and lively word, and rightly and duly administer thy holy Sacraments."

May God grant you great joy and laughter too as you go about the work of ministry this week. (September 27, 2004)

PASTORAL WISDOM

Recently I wrote to our retired pastors asking them to share with me their best insights on the work of pastoral ministry. In their years of ministry, what had they found to be the essential qualities for faithful pastors?

I have received more than fifty wonderful responses. They represent at least two millennia of wisdom! Here are some recurring themes in their responses.

1. Successful pastoral ministry requires not only theological ability, biblical fidelity, and a good personality; it requires hard work! Pastors must be "self-starters" who proactively engage their parishioners and their communities by knocking on doors, engaging in conversation, making contacts, and other efforts to reach people. Disciplined, determined work is required.

2. Faithful pastors must have a vivid sense of vocation, a sense of being summoned by God to do this work. The work that pastors do is too demanding to do it for any other reason than the conviction that one is called to do this work, that God wants you to do it.

3. The only enduring reasons for being in ministry are theological. Pastors must constantly refurbish their sense that this is a "God thing," that ministry is more than a mere "helping profession." Pastoral ministry arises out of theological commitments and is dependent upon what God is doing in the church and the world.

4. Though some seem to believe that pastoral visitation is outmoded, there is no substitute for meeting people where they live, for offering yourself to them through visiting in their homes and businesses.

5. Pastoral ministry is relational. Your people must believe that you care about them, that you know them individually, and that you are trying to love them.

I find these to be enduring insights about ministry, gleaned from many years of collective wisdom. I share these with you in the hope that you will be inspired as I have been by our retired pastors. (May 5, 2008)

NOTE

1. Alexander Dru, ed., *The Journals of Kierkegaard* (New York: Harper Torchbooks, 1958), 205.

CHAPTER 14

THE CRAFT OF PREACHING

MATTHEW'S MEANING

This past week we had a wonderful Bishop's Convocation that focused on the ministry of preaching. For those of us who get our texts from the Common Lectionary, 2008 is Year A, and Matthew is the Gospel. What would a church such as ours be like if the only Gospel we had was the Gospel of Matthew?

For one thing, it would be a church in which the Christian Education program ran everything. Matthew's church wouldn't have a pipe organ or stained glass windows. It would be a lecture hall for giving and receiving instruction. There would be lectures, lots of them, because here is a Gospel that believes in education because it believes disciples can actually understand what Jesus is getting at and they can grow in their faith.

In Matthew 13, Jesus tells the very same parable about the seeds and the soil that he told in Mark. In Mark, nobody got the point. The disciples admitted that they didn't get it and, even after Jesus explained it, there is no reason to believe that they understood. But here in Matthew, when Jesus asks, "Have you understood?" the disciples respond with a resounding, "Yes!"

You can find hundreds of books in our seminary libraries on the parables, each with a different, often confusing interpretation of the parables of Jesus. But here in Matthew, these fishermen and former IRS agents understand those stories that the scholars don't get!

Matthew depicts Jesus as a sort of rabbi surrounded by his attentive, comprehending students. This Gospel is very practical, full of instruction for how to get along as a disciple in everyday life. The Sermon on the Mount tells you what to do when some-one asks you to carry a burden for a mile, or how to respond when someone strikes you on the cheek. What Jesus instructs us to do may not be easy, but at least it is understandable.

Matthew opens Advent 2007 with Joseph, a man who has been introduced to us as "righteous." He is one who is a righteous son of Israel, which means that he studies the Torah and the rab-binical interpretations of Torah. Because of his righteousness, Joseph knows just the right Scripture verse for every situation in life.

One night an angel comes to Joseph to tell him that his fiancée is pregnant, and not by him. What is a righteous man like Joseph to do? Put her away. Put her away with compassion, of course, but get rid of her.

No, the angel tells Joseph. There is an even higher "righteous-ness" than that so wonderfully enshrined in Torah. He is to take Mary as a wife and to name the child Jesus, which means "God saves."

How does God save in this Gospel? Through the gift of Jesus, true, but Jesus must be a gift that is received, accepted by ordinary people like Mary and Joseph, who find their little lives caught up in a higher righteousness. Joseph hears, he understands, he obeys.

There is good news here for struggling disciples. Here the gospel is no unattainable, impossible ideal. Rather the gospel is a way, a path that is intended to be walked by those who obedi-ently respond to what they hear and see in Jesus; this sounds like a very Wesleyan idea to me.

Matthew 25 ends with the parable of the Last Judgment, the apocalypse in which the judge separates all the nations of the earth. On what basis? On the basis of how well these sheep responded to the "least of these" in concrete, tangible ways, in the little things like a visitation in prison or a cup of water.

In Matthew we are allowed to listen in, to overhear Jesus as he instructs his disciples. He is speaking to those who follow him as the new Moses, the new guide, the new teacher. Evangelism involves not cranking down the Christian way to the lowest common denominator, but rather allowing outsiders, non-disciples, to listen in on Jesus' instruction to his disciples.

For some time now I have been fascinated by how much of a pastor's time is expended in educating the congregation. The day is over, if it ever was, when we lived in a basically "Christian" culture where people got this faith by osmosis, by drinking the water and breathing the air and being lucky enough to be born in Illinois. Now, there is a new emphasis on Christian formation, on the making of Christians.

The lively congregations I know of in North Alabama are those that place this educational, formational ministry at the center of the congregation's life together. In most of our congregations we are dealing with a high percentage of folk who have been either unformed or malformed in the faith. A new generation of disciples is appreciative of those pastors who take their struggle to live the faith seriously.

In Matthew, Jesus loves his followers enough to teach them, to help them make their way in the world, to give them the intellectual and spiritual equipment they need to be faithful. Many people in our day are in difficulty, not because of some psychic problem, not because of some negative childhood experience. They are simply confused. They haven't taken the time and the trouble to think through the faith, to place their lives and their issues in the context of the gospel. Jesus loves to do that in this Gospel. Matthew is therefore a great Gospel for the church in our time and place.

Tom Long tells of finishing a lecture in a Presbyterian church and looking up to see a large woman moving at full sail down the aisle toward him with a determined, tough look on her face. He braced himself. "Do you teach in a seminary?" she asked. "Yes,"

129

Tom replied in a shaking voice. "Well, I want you to teach your seminarians in such a way that they take us seriously!" she said.

Matthew takes struggling disciples seriously with practical guidance for following Jesus. The gospel is not some heroic, impossible, esoteric mystery for the enlightened. The gospel is a way of life, a way of walking along with Jesus and listening to Jesus, then attempting to embody Jesus' way in all that we do.

This is therefore a great year to be preaching from Matthew. (October 15, 2007)

PREACHING: CHARACTER AND CREDIBILITY

Our Bishop's Convocation takes place this week, when the pastors of our Conference will be focusing on the ministry of preaching. Dr. Thomas G. Long of Emory will lead us. For the next few weeks my Bishop's messages will reflect on the task of preaching.

When Aristotle was offering in his *Rhetoric* the "available means of persuasion," including reason, emotion, and the *character of the speaker*, he listed the character of the speaker as the most important. In fact, a later rhetorician would define a good speech as "a good person speaking well." The credibility of the speaker continues to be one of the most powerful aspects of a persuasive speech. Sermons appeal to the emotions, appeal to reason, cite Scripture, and use story. However, both the opinions of classical rhetoric and contemporary studies of public speaking agree that the personality, the character of the speaker, is the key factor in the credibility of the speech.

Even though credibility is a gift offered by the audience to the speaker, that does not mean the speaker has no control over credibility. At least five factors influence the credibility of a speaker:

1. *Character*. The speaker must be perceived as trustworthy and true. There must be congruence between the listeners' assessment of the personality of the speaker and

what the speaker is saying. Parish pastors have great opportunity to influence through character. Listeners get to know you intimately in the daily activity of the congregation. Of course this can be a two-edged sword! Because they know you so well in their daily interaction with you as their pastor, congregants are apt to pick up phoniness, artificiality, and incongruence between what you say and who they perceive you to be.

2. *Competence.* Your audience must perceive you as a person who has control over the subject.

3. *Composure.* Speakers who are nervous are less trustworthy than speakers who appear confident and composed.

4. *Likeability.* We listen attentively and positively to people for whom we have positive feelings. This can be a great challenge for the Christian communicator. After all, to be faithful to the gospel, at times we must say things that are not likeable, ideas and beliefs that will challenge our hearers, things that our hearers hear as criticism. Nevertheless, if our hearers are positively disposed toward us as people, they will receive even our criticism much better than they would if they were negatively inclined toward us.

5. *Extroversion.* Speakers who reach out to their audience are positively perceived by their audience. The audience perceives that the speaker really cares about them, really wants to be heard by them. However, extroverts in public speaking also note that it is possible to be too extroverted. A speaker who seems too intent on pleasing an audience, on being liked by the audience, can be perceived by the audience as disingenuous and artificial. The audience, feeling that the speaker is putting the make upon them, may resist the speaker. Defenses rise when we feel we are about to be manipulated by another person for that person's own ends.

Although most preachers do not stand up and enumerate for the congregation all of their academic degrees and all of the schools where they have studied, we will say things like, "This week, in my study of today's Scripture, I had a tough task before me." Or we will say, "In my twenty years as a pastor, I have found that...."

Conversely, credibility can be engendered by the speaker admitting to his or her shortcomings. The speaker says, "One of my weaknesses is I tend to judge people by their appearance. I will see someone shabbily dressed, and I think that this person is rather shabby. Have you ever done that?" Preachers are sometimes perceived by their congregations as people who have solved all spiritual problems for themselves and are now, from their exalted perch of perfectionism, seeking to instruct the congregation. Letting some of our humanity come through in our speech is a means of establishing greater credibility.

"We have this treasure in earthen vessels," says Paul. We preachers are thoroughly human vessels, yet God has given us a treasure to communicate to our people. One way we communicate is through who we are. Character and credibility are thus closely linked. (October 8, 2007)

FOR GOD'S SAKE SAY IT

When I was courting the Rev. Carl Parker's daughter (who eventually became my wife, Patsy), Mr. Parker was serving as a District Superintendent in the Marion District of the Methodist Church. I was nervous. I wanted to make a good impression. I was considering entering seminary in the fall, and I wanted the approval of this preacher's family.

Because a District Superintendent does not serve one congregation but supervises those preachers in the district, Mr. Parker spent many Sundays in the pew rather than in the pulpit, a situation that he detested. On one particular Sunday, the preacher was a master of ambiguity and equivocation. Mr. Parker squirmed in his pew as the preacher carefully qualified just about every statement made in the sermon. At five-minute intervals throughout the sermon, Mr. Parker withdrew his large railroad watch from his pocket, the watch that had been given to him by some thankful congregation of the past. He would gaze at his watch, remain surprised that so little time had passed, close it, shake his head, thrust it back into his pocket, and groan slightly.

The poor preacher continued to flail away, thrashing at his subject, rather than delivering it. "We need to be more committed to Christ...but not to the point of fanaticism, not to the point of neglect of our other important responsibilities. We need to have a greater dedication to the work of the church. Now I don't mean that the church is the only significant organization of which you are a member. Most of us have obligations to various community groups...." And on, and on.

After service, all of us in the District Superintendent's party brushed right past Mr. Milk Toast with barely a word of greeting. Mr. Parker led us down the sidewalk back to the district parsonage, like ducks in a row. He went right through the front door and charged up the stairs. Pausing midway, he whirled around, shaking a finger at me and thundering, "Young man, if God should be calling you into the pastoral ministry, and if you should ever be given a church by the bishop, and if God ever gives you a word to say, *for God's sake would you say it!*"

Mainline Protestantism seems to be suffering from a failure of theological nerve. Our trumpets suffer from our uncertain sound—the bland leading the bland. Courage to speak arises, in great part, from the conviction that God has given us something to say. I recall Leander Keck (in a debate on the most effective sermon styles) saying, "When the messenger is gripped by a Message, the messenger will find the means to speak it." As preachers, we know the challenge in a relativistic culture of standing up and saying, "This news is good, this word is true."

On one occasion Walter Brueggemann said, "If you are a coward by nature, don't worry. We can still use you. You can get down behind the biblical text. You can peek out from behind the text, saying, 'I don't know if I would say this, but I do think the text does.'" I like that image—the preacher hunkered down, taking cover behind the biblical text, speaking a word not of the preacher's devising.

Courage to speak requires clarity about our source of authority. If we only stand in the pulpit to "share ourselves" or to "tell my story," as some misguided recent homiletics have urged us, then the church shall end, not with a bang but in a simpering sigh after a thousand qualifications and reservations.

This Sunday, take Mr. Parker's advice. If God gives you a word for God's people, *for God's sake, say it!* (January 29, 2007)

ON NOT REACHING OUR CULTURE THROUGH OUR PREACHING

Recently I led a group of pastors in a discussion about our preaching. When I asked the pastors, "What areas would you like help with in your preaching?" most of them responded with, "I want help in making connections with my listeners, relating the gospel to their everyday lives."

"I want to preach sermons which really hit my people where they live."

In sum, these pastors wanted to preach in a way that addressed their culture. There was a time when I would have agreed that this was one of the primary purposes of Christian preaching— to relate the gospel to contemporary culture. However, I have come to question this way of construing the task of Christian preaching.

Sometimes in leaning over to speak to the modern world, I fear that we may have fallen in! When we sought to use our sermons to build a bridge from the old world of the Bible to the new modern world, the traffic was only moving in one direction on that interpretive bridge. It was always the modern world rummaging about in Scripture, saying things like "This relates to me," or, "I'm sorry, this is really impractical," or, "I really can't make sense out of that." It was always the modern world telling the Bible what's what.

I don't believe that the Bible wants to "speak to the modern world." Rather, I think the Bible wants to change it, to convert it. The modern world is not only the realm of the telephone, the computer, and allegedly "critical thinking"; this world is also the habitat of Auschwitz, two of the bloodiest wars of history, and assorted totalitarian schemes that have consumed the lives of millions. Why would our preaching want to be comprehensible to *that* world? Too often Christians have treated the modern world as if it is an unalterable fact, a reality to which we were obligated to adjust and adapt, rather than a point of view with which we might argue.

Fortunately, modern ways of knowing and thinking are gradually losing their privileged status in Western thought. We are realizing that modernity is only one way of describing what is going on in the world. Humanity has received many gifts from modern, scientific, technological ways of thinking. However, as we ended the twentieth century we realized that modernity was not without its losses.

Rather than reaching out to speak to our culture, I think our time as preachers is better spent inculturating twenty-first-century Americans into that culture which is called church. There is no way that I can crank the gospel down to the level where any American can walk in off the street and know what it is all about within fifteen minutes. One can't even do that with baseball! You have to learn the vocabulary, the rules, and the culture in order to understand it. Being in church is something at least as different as baseball.

Forming the church through our speech, laying on contemporary Christians the stories, images, and practices which make us disciples, is our most challenging task as preachers. The point is not to speak to the culture. The point is to change it. God's appointed means of producing change is called church. God's typical way of producing church is called preaching. (November 5, 2007)

CHAPTER 15

APOCALYPTIC RIFF

TO: THE CHURCH CALLED MAINLINE

A few years ago the editors of Christianity Today *had a special issue on the book of Revelation. They asked some of us to write imaginary "letters" to our various church families like Pentecostal, Charismatic, Evangelical, and so on; I was asked to write a letter to Mainline Protestantism. Here was my tongue-in-cheek response:*

To: The Church Called Mainline

Behold I make all things new! Even you.

How eagerly you began this century that you so confidently called "Christian." You organized to beat the Devil, to build, to expand, to crusade, to reform, to grow; quite a contrast to the way your century ends. You, who enjoyed thinking of yourselves as "mainline," got sidelined. Though you are averse to taking my word literally, for my sake, and for yours, I hope that you will at least take these words seriously.

I, the One who so exuberantly turned water into wine at Cana, tire of your propensity to turn wine to water at your bureaucracies in Nashville, Minneapolis, and Louisville. The best thing about you is your past. What does that tell you? My, how you loved

137

to organize and build! You made North America into the most thoroughly Protestant Christian place in the world: hospitals, orphanages, schools, nursing homes, and printing presses. You really took love of neighbor to a new level and I'm grateful. And while I enjoyed dismantling sacred edifices rather than building them, you built some beautiful churches. Give me *The Lutheran Hymnal* any day over most of those tasteless "praise choruses" of some of my evangelicals.

Fosdick, Harkness, Peale, Steimlie, Thurman, Achtemeier can preach for me any time they like. I wish some of them would steer a bit closer to the Scriptures, but I'll speak to them individually about that. When you mainliners stop talking about me, your preaching tends to get moralistic and trite. I hate that. It would-n't kill you to get back to the Bible.

You know me, I love to make the oldline new. If you will stick with me, I shall give you a future, new wineskins and all that. I am Lord of Life, not death. I shall move you from mordant decline to life. I've still got plans for you. You'll be smaller, but small can be good. Ask the Mennonites. You will no longer be in charge of the nation, if you ever were. Remember, the national church thing was your idea of church, not mine. Get back to basics like worship, service, and witness. Don't mourn the down-sizing of your bureaucracy. You were once good at mission. Now that much of North America has never heard of me, it's about time to start thinking of yourselves as missionaries.

Your marginalization may be providential.

I promise you renewal, not restoration. Many will be grateful for your mainline open-handedness: the way you manage to make room for such a wide range of faithfulness within your congrega-tions, your confidence that the church is more than an isolated congregation, that I ought to have a Body, and that the witness of the saints is worth celebrating today. Personally, I think that you tend to be open-minded to a fault. Latitudinarianism is you all over. I wish you would hire some theologians with some guts for a change. Can't you find something more fun to do than General Assembly, General Conference, and Diocesan

Conventions? Some of your good ideas from the last century may need a decent burial if I can work birth in you in the next.

One more thing. Please get out of the middle of the road! That's where all the accidents happen, theologically speaking.

Remember, I wasn't crucified for my moderation. (May 9, 2005)